John R. Kelso

Spiritualism Sustained

John R. Kelso

Spiritualism Sustained

ISBN/EAN: 9783337334765

Printed in Europe, USA, Canada, Australia, Japan

Cover: Foto ©Lupo / pixelio.de

More available books at **www.hansebooks.com**

Spiritualism Sustained

—IN—

FIVE LECTURES.

—BY—

JOHN R. KELSO, A. M.

NEW YORK:
PRINTED AT THE TRUTH SEEKER OFFICE,
33 CLINTON PLACE.

CONTENTS.

LECTURE.   PAGE.

I. SPIRITUALISM SUSTAINED BY THE BIBLE, . 7

II. SPIRITUALISM SUSTAINED BY THE CHRISTIAN CHURCH, ... 50

III. SPIRITUALISM A NECESSITY IN GOD'S GENERAL GOVERNMENT, ... 102

IV. SPIRITUAL MEDIUMSHIP, ... 156

V. OBJECTIONS TO SPIRITUALISM ANSWERED, . 204

PREFACE.

Confidently believing that, notwithstanding its many admitted imperfections, this little book is calculated to do much good, the author has no apology to offer for placing it before the world. All that he has to say is: "Let it stand or fall upon its own merit!" If, in the estimation of the intelligent and progressive minds of the present age, it possess real merit, it will stand; if not, it will fall. This is just as it should be. Will those whose decision is in its favor please help place it before the world?

THE AUTHOR.

SPIRITUALISM SUSTAINED.

LECTURE I.

SPIRITUALISM SUSTAINED BY THE BIBLE.

As you are doubtless all well aware, Spiritualism rests upon what its advocates regard as two grand and well established truths. The first of these truths is: "That man, after the dissolution of the body, continues still to exist as a conscious and intelligent being." The second is: "That disembodied men, called spirits, can, under certain conditions, and frequently do, in various ways, carry on intelligible correspondence with persons still in the body."

In some form, the first of these truths is almost universally accepted by every nation and every tribe of the world. In my present lecture, therefore, I shall omit any further notice of it, and give my entire attention to the proving of the second truth, that of spiritual communications. In proving these communications to be facts, I shall give the only positive proofs that can possibly be given of man's immortality as a conscious individual.

The doctrine of spiritual communications is peculiar to Spiritualists, and a belief in this doctrine constitutes a man a Spiritualist, even though he may disclaim the appellation, and though he may be a member of an orthodox church.* Indeed, there are many Spiritualists among the members of every religious denomination of the world.

Though the claims of Spiritualism can all be fully established without the evidence of the Bible, yet there are many persons who, on this subject, will receive nothing as evidence unless it comes from the Bible. For the benefit of this class of persons, therefore, I propose, in my present lecture, to prove by the Bible the truth of every phase of Spiritualism. In doing this I shall compel these persons to either reject the evidence of the Bible and to thus become Infidels, or to admit the truths of Spiritualism and to thus become Spiritualists. In either of these cases my object will have been accomplished. They will have been freed from the slavish mental chains in which priestcraft has so long held them bound, and will have taken their places in the ranks of the grand army of Liberalism.

You may object, however, that, after having written and published a large work for the express purpose of proving the Bible to be totally unworthy of belief, I have no right to use its testimony as evidence in the present case. To this objection I reply that the Bible is your own witness—the only witness whose testimony in this case you will receive as evidence; and, since I can win my case on the testimony of your witness alone, I have an indisputable right to do so. I shall not, therefore, impeach the testimony of your witness in this case, no matter what I may think of his credibility. I shall show that his testimony, if accepted, fully establishes the truths of

Spiritualism, and then let you impeach that testimony, if you wish to do so. In short, I propose, for the sake of the argument, to concede all that you claim for the Bible and for the God of the Bible—in whose real existence I have not a particle of faith—and then, on your own ground and with your own weapons, to gain over you a complete victory for the glorious cause of Spiritualism.

I wish, in the first place, to determine, so far as possible, the nature of those personages so often mentioned in the Bible, called angels. These personages play a conspicuous part, not only in the religion of the Jews, but also in that of the Christians. In order, then, to correctly understand the history of either of these religions, it becomes absolutely indispensable that we know exactly what those angels were; or, rather, what they are, since they are supposed to be still in existence. They have generally been assumed to constitute a distinct order of intelligences higher than that of man This assumption, however, as I shall clearly prove, is not well founded. I shall prove that the personages called angels in the Bible were neither more nor less than human beings, some of whom were still in the body, while others were in the form of spirits. I shall also prove that, if the angels of the Bible were, in any respect, superior to other human beings, their superiority consisted, not in a higher nature, but simply in a higher condition—in higher attainments or in higher official importance.

In regard to the origin of angels there exists, among theologians, a great diversity of opinions. Some conjecture that angels were created long before the creation of the world and of man. Others hold, and correctly, too, as I shall soon show, that angels were included in the six-days' creation of which the Bible gives an account. These are the two most common opinions in regard to this matter.

The reason assigned for the former of these two opinions is that, otherwise, God must have been utterly alone and totally unemployed during the entire eternity that must, of necessity, have preceded the creation of the material universe. Those who entertain this opinion, however, overlook the important fact that, by their assumption, they merely place these difficulties further back without tending in the least to remove them. They overlook the important fact that, if angels were ever created at all, the period of time which has elapsed since their creation, be it ever so immense, is, nevertheless, undeniably a finite period, and that this finite period, taken from the infinite period of God's existence, must, of necessity, leave undiminished an infinite period still beyond. Indeed, there can be no assignable point in the past, whether it be that at which men were created, or angels, or anything else, beyond which infinite duration does not still extend. No finite period, taken from that infinite period, can possibly render the latter any the less; and no finite period, added to that infinite period, can possibly render the latter any the greater. In short, it is an indisputable fact that no change of any kind can possibly be made in an infinite period. No matter, then, how long ago God may have created the angels, he must, of absolute necessity, have existed just as long previous to their creation as he has existed previous to the present time. In any possible view of the case, then, God must, of absolute necessity, have spent an utterly endless, and yet an actually ended, period of duration, utterly alone and unemployed, previous to the point at which he began the creation of anything at all. With the ideas that now generally prevail in regard to duration no one can deny the truth of this last statement, and yet, as you clearly perceive, it involves a palpable absurdity, an utter impossibility, affecting the very existence of God himself. In previous works, "Deity Analyzed" and "The Bible Analyzed," I have much more fully considered this matter, and in a future work, "The Universe Analyzed," I shall consider it still further, giving some entirely original and, as I believe, very valuable ideas of what is called duration. At present I can give the subject no further notice.

As I have already stated, other theologians hold that angels, like man and the lower animals, were made during the six days in which "the Lord made heaven and earth, the sea, and all that in them is." If angels are human beings, this view is undeniably the correct one. Indeed, it is bound to be the correct view any way. Since all the things that are in heaven, or on the earth, or in the sea, were made at that time, and since all who believe in the existence of angels at all admit that they are either in heaven or on earth, they are bound to have been included in the "all" that were made at that time. If, then, they be a distinct and higher order of beings, is it not very strange that man, and even the birds, the beasts, the creeping things, the plants, etc., should all be distinctly mentioned as being created at that time, and not a word said about angels? Is it reasonable to assume that the highest creature of all made on that occasion was thus entirely overlooked? Besides this, the Bible certainly represents man as the masterpiece made on that occasion—as being more like God than was any other creature. And how could this be if the angels, who were created at the same time, were a still higher order of beings than was man, and still more like God? This becomes still more strange, too, when we consider that, according to all orthodox teachings, angels all derive their origin from direct creation, and not, like man and other living creatures, from a single original pair, through the process of procreation or parentage. On this hypothesis countless legions of angels must have been manufactured all at once on that memorable occasion. This marked exception to the general rule of creation observed on that occasion, had it really existed, would surely have been noticed in a special manner.

Besides all this, according to the teachings of all orthodox theologians, the angels are all males, all chronic old bachelors, no such things as angelesses being known among them. There being no females among them probably accounts for the fact that they are so good and so happy. Why could not men have been made on that same plan? And yet, on the hypothesis that all things exhibit marks of design, of what design, in the total absence of all females, does the male sex of those angels exhibit the marks? Since all the living creatures mentioned in the Bible account of creation were made male and female, and were commanded to increase and multiply, these angelic old bachelors again formed so marked an exception to the general rule that they should certainly have been noticed in a special manner. It may be, however, that, in consequence of the rawness of the material of which himself had just been manufactured, Adam's brain was a little muddy, and that, when he saw the new-made mud birds and the equally new-made mud angels all flopping around together, trying to fly, he mistook them all for birds, and hence failed to notice angels as a distinct order of beings. This assumption removes every difficulty and is fully as reasonable as are any of those advanced in favor of an origin for angels distinct from that of men. Be all this as it may, however, the angels, as I have already shown, certainly must have been included in the Bible's six-days' creation. To attempt, therefore, to place the creation of angels outside of those six days would be to contradict the Bible and to involve yourselves in inextricable difficulties and absurdities, which, however, I cannot now notice.

And to admit that the angels were included in the Bible's six-days' creation, and yet, at the same time, to assume that they were made a distinct order of intelligences, would, as we have just seen, involve you in equally insurmountable difficulties. On this assumption you cannot possibly explain why angels were never seen or even heard of until men had become spirits. You will notice that, before any men had become spirits, God in person bore all of his own messages to mankind, and in person received all the messages of mankind to himself. Afterwards, however, you will also notice, he had all of these messages borne by angels, who invariably appeared in the human form, and who were generally called men. And now, how can you account for these facts, except on the hypothesis that God had no angels or messengers until he had human spirits to serve him in that capacity.

Theologians have also differed very widely as to whether angels do or do not have bodies. One of the councils of Nice, in 787, voted them an ethereal body, but this was taken from them by a majority vote of the Lateran council of 1215, and it was made a capital offense to teach that they had bodies of any kind. Whether they have, or have not, bodies, I do not now care to discuss. In fact, it makes no difference. It is sufficient for my purpose to prove that they are human beings.

The word angel is derived, with very little change of form, from the Greek, and means simply a messenger or a minister. It conveys no idea of superiority beyond that of official importance. Indeed, angels appear originally to have been mere personifications of natural forces, special providences, and even of inanimate material objects. As we now, by personification, speak of a pestilence, a thunderbolt, or a cannon ball, as a messenger of death, so by the same figure of speech, the ancients spoke of such things as angels of death. When the term angel was applied to persons, it was to those only who were acting as messengers, ministers, agents, etc., and then it imported their office or occupation and not their origin or nature. Any man, whether in the body or in the spirit form, became an angel the moment he became a messenger, a minister, etc., and ceased to be an angel the moment he ceased to act in such capacity. He was an angel of the king, an angel of the church, an angel of the Lord, an angel of the devil, an angel of death, etc., according to the party in whose service he was acting, or the kind of occupation in which he was engaged. Men and angels are spoken of in the Bible just as men and messengers are spoken of among ourselves. That I am correct in this is a fact well known to every one who is at all acquainted with the Greek language.

In the eighteenth and nineteenth chapters of Genesis we have an account of three persons who displayed wonderful powers, foretelling future events, striking whole crowds of men with blindness, destroying cities with fire from heaven, etc., and yet who, a part of the time, are called men, and a part of the time angels. First the one of these terms is applied to them and then the other. The writer evidently considers the two terms synonymous, so far as the nature of the individuals to whom he applies them is concerned. Sometimes he speaks of those individuals in their official or professional capacity, and then, of course, he calls them angels; this term being used, as I have already stated, to indicate the official or professional capacity of persons, and never for any other purpose. At other times he speaks of them in their private or personal capacity, and then, of course, he calls them men; this term being used to indicate the nature or order of the beings to whom it is applied and never for any other purpose. This use of the two terms is entirely proper, if angels are men, and men, when acting as messengers, ministers, etc., are angels. If, however, men and angels are different orders of beings, an angel cannot be a man, nor can a man be an angel. On this hypothesis the Bible speaks falsely when it declares that the individuals in question were men, and, at the same time, angels. As well might it declare that a certain animal was a monkey, and, at the same time, an elephant. Will you bring the charge of falsehood against the Bible? If not, are you not compelled to admit that those three angels were human beings—the spirits of men—and that they gave some wonderful spiritual manifestations?

That those three angels were men is still further proved by the fact that they had forms like the forms of men; that they had voices like the voices of men; that, in walking, their feet became soiled, as do the feet of men; that they grew weary and hungry and thirsty after the manner of men; that they ate and drank as do men; that they used the same kinds of food and drink as are used by men; that they sought shelter from the heat of the sun as do men; that they talked and reasoned as do men; that they slept in houses as do men; that, in every respect, they resembled men. If, then, they were not men, as the Bible says they were, what were they and in what respect did they differ from men? If that portion of the story be false which declares that those three angels were men, may not the whole story be equally false?

In Genesis xxxii we have an account of a wrestling match between Jacob and a heavenly being—God's messenger or representative—and yet the Bible calls this being a man, and has Jacob, after a long tussle, beat him in the wrestling match. If that heavenly being was a man—a human spirit—was not this affair a wonderful spiritual manifestation? Was not materialization exhibited in it to perfection? Was not Jacob a remarkable spiritual medium? And was not this spiritual manifestation made by a good spirit through a good medium? Is not the same true of the wonderful spiritual manifestations, already described, made by the three men-angels to Abraham? What can you say, in these two remarkable cases, against either the mediums who received the communications or the spirits who sent them? Dare you say that the angels mentioned in these two cases were not men, when the Bible says they were? And dare you, with these two cases before you, declare that all Spiritualism is of the devil? Had the devil anything to do in these two cases?

In Acts xxiii we have an account of a fierce dissension which Paul, for his own safety, excited between the Pharisees, who believed in the existence of angels and of other spirits, and the Sadducees, who denied the existence of both. The ninth verse says: "And there arose a great cry; and the scribes that were of the Pharisees' part arose, and strove, saying, We find no evil in this man, but if a spirit or an angel hath spoken to him, let us not fight against God." This shows plainly enough that all of those Jews who believed in the existence of angels and spirits at all, believed that both could, and that both did, sometimes appear unto men and converse with them. It also shows that those Spiritualistic Jews believed that spirits and angels were the same, or were, at least, so nearly alike that a man could not well distinguish between them. They did not doubt that Paul had seen a spirit of some kind. Their only doubt was as to whether that spirit was an angel or official spirit, or whether it was an ordinary, unofficial spirit. They also regarded all opposition to spiritual communications as fighting "against God." How unlike the so-called orthodox of the present day, who, in opposing similar spiritual phenomena, claim to be fighting against the devil. The Sadducees also regarded angels and spirits as the same, and in denying the existence of the one, they were bound to deny the existence of the other.

Matthew says that when certain women went to the sepulcher of Jesus they saw there an angel who informed them that Jesus had risen from the dead. Mark declares that this angel was a young man. Luke says there were two angels, and John says these two angels were two men. These two men were in shining garments, from which fact we may know that they were disembodied men, or spirits. And now, I ask, were those bright beings, at the same time, both men and angels, the two terms being equally applicable to them? If not, do not two of the Evangelists lie in declaring that they were angels, when they were not; or the other two, in declaring that they were men, when they were not? If angels and men are distinct orders of beings, it is impossible for the assertions of both sets of Evangelists to be true. Dare you, then, deny that men and angels are the same by nature? If you dare do this, then which set of Evangelists are guilty of lying?

If, by nature, men and angels are the same, then all the Evangelists equally speak the truth. Two of them speak of the bright beings in question, in their official capacity, and, of course, call them angels.

The other two speak of them in their private capacity, and, of course, call them men.

On that same occasion, so Matthew informs us, many other spirits made their appearance, but those at the sepulcher, being the only ones acting as messengers, were the only ones that were called angels, or that could have been so called. These angels, then, were simply human spirits on duty as messengers; and this fact proves not only the truth of Spiritualism, but also its acceptance in the sight of Heaven— its adoption by God himself as the means by which to usher in the Christian Dispensation. I defy any escape from these conclusions without a total rejection of the whole story of the resurrection of Jesus.

In Mark xii, 25, Jesus declares that in the resurrection men "are as the angels which are in heaven." Can men be "as the angels" and still be different from them? In Luke xx, 36, Jesus, speaking of resurrected men or spirits, declares that "they are equal unto the angels." Being "as the angels which are in heaven," and "equal unto" them, cannot human spirits communicate with men and do all other things that can be done by angels? If you admit that they can, you indorse in full all the claims of Spiritualism. If you deny that they can, you deny that they "are as the angels which are in heaven," and "equal unto" them. By this denial you make Jesus a liar. Shall we believe him or you?

In Rev. xxii, 8, 9, we read: "And I, John, saw these things and heard them. And when I had heard and seen, I fell down to worship before the feet of the angel which showed me these things. Then saith he unto me, See thou do it not: for I am thy fellow servant, and of thy brethren the prophets, and of them which keep the sayings of this book : Worship God." This angel, then, was certainly a human spirit. From preceding chapters we learn that this was one of seven angels of the same order, and that he possessed as wonderful powers as are ascribed to any other angels mentioned in the whole Bible. Here, then, were seven angels, of a very high order, who were human spirits, or at least one of them was a human spirit, and he was equal, in every respect, to any one of the others.

On another occasion, as we learn from Rev. xix, 10, John, in his refreshing simplicity and wonderful religious zeal, attempted to worship another angel, who was thus constrained to declare himself one of John's brethren, and, of course, a human spirit. In the preceding chapter we learn that this angel was also possessed of "great power," and "that the earth was lightened with his glory." This human spirit, then, was an angel pre-eminently great and glorious. With these examples before you, can you deny that Jesus spake the truth when he declared that human spirits "are as the angels which are in heaven," and "equal unto" them? These two angels, being the only ones that John attempted to worship, were the only ones that had any occasion to declare their nature. Had he attempted to worship any of the other angels with whom he conversed, he would doubtless have learned from their own lips that they, too, were of his "brethren the prophets, and of them which keep the sayings of this book." At any rate, I defy you to point out in the whole Bible a single instance in which any angel ascribed to himself any other than a human nature and a human origin. I will further defy you to point out in the whole Bible a single passage from which, when taken with its context, it can be fairly inferred that angels have any other than a human nature and a human origin.

In Rev. xxi, 17, we read: "And he measured the wall thereof, an hundred and forty and four cubits, according to the measure of a man, that is, of the angel." Here John informs us that the measure was that of a man, and that the man was the angel of whom he had just been speaking. Does not this make the angel a man and the man an angel? If in some other writing we should read: "The wall was a hundred and forty-four yards long, according to the measurement of a man of our party, that is, of the guide," would we not understand the man to be a guide, and the guide to be a man? And is not this supposed case an exact parallel to that given by John? If then, in the one case, the guide be a man, is not the angel, in the other case, bound to be a man also?

In 1 Cor. vi, 3, Paul says: "Know ye not that we shall judge angels?" Could we judge a superior order of beings? Could we judge any but human beings? In the eleventh chapter of this same book Paul requires the women to cover their heads in church, "because of the angels." Few passages of scripture have caused theologians more perplexity than has this. They cannot see any good reason why the women of that church, or of any other, should have been required to cover their heads "because of the angels." With their views of angels there would be no reason for such a requirement. If, however, they will consider that those angels were simply messengers, or ministers, from other churches, the difficulty will at once disappear.

Many of those messengers were probably from countries in Asia, where none but lewd women were wont to go uncovered in public. These messengers, or angels, as they were called, would have been shocked to see a church filled with uncovered women. To them it would have appeared like a vast house of ill fame. Indeed, as we learn from other portions of the same chapter, it was a house of very doubtful fame. This church was at Corinth, and there, as in Asia, the women, especially if married, were wont to go veiled, or covered, in public. The members of this church, however, as Paul informs us, were accustomed to meet, in the name of the Lord, for the purpose of eating, drinking, and carousing. To such an extent had they carried their pious dissipation that, from "this cause," many of them had become weak and sickly, and many others had already died untimely deaths. Demoralized by such a life, the women, it seems, had begun to go uncovered in their meetings, and had thus brought reproach upon the church. For this Paul reproves them, and, in substance, lets them know that, if they have no regard for the opinions of those among whom they live, they ought, at least, to respect the feelings and the opinions of the messengers and ministers—"the angels"—from other churches, who, like himself, having never been accustomed to see respectable women go uncovered, could not become reconciled to this innovation.

As a reason for his instructions on this subject

Paul refers, not to such views as the inhabitants of heaven might be supposed to entertain in regard to the wearing of the hair and of head-dresses, but to the well-known prejudices of the men of that time and of that country. Read the whole chapter, and you will see that my conclusions are all correct.

These angels, then, were simply living men from other churches. Being messengers, or ministers, they were, of course, called angels. Spoken of in their official capacity they could not, in Greek, have been called anything else. The same is bound to be true also of the seven angels of the seven churches, of Ephesus, Pergamus, etc. These angels were simply the ministers in charge of those churches. Dr. Clarke admits this, as do nearly all other theologians whose opinions are worthy of notice. To suppose anything else, indeed, than that those angels were the living ministers of the several churches named, involves more absurdities and difficulties than theologians have ever been able to explain away.

If, however, you reject my views, and hold that all these angels were spirits from heaven, you give Spiritualism a good indorsement, for then you have such spirits among us, taking a lively interest in our affairs, even intermeddling in the fashions of our women and communicating to certain chronic old bachelors, like Paul, their objections to certain styles of female head-gear and their preference for others. Without such communications Paul could not have known how the angels wished the women of Corinth to wear their hair and to dress their heads. You thus make Paul a spiritual medium, receiving and imparting spiritual communications, such as you would stigmatize as ridiculous if gravely reported and acted upon by Spiritualists of the present time.

In the thirteenth chapter of Judges we have an account of an angel of God who declared himself a man. The eleventh verse says: "And Manoah arose, and went after his wife, and came to the man, and said unto him, Art thou the man that spakest unto the woman? And he said, I am." This angel, then, was a man, or, rather, a human spirit. That he was not a man in the body we learn from the twentieth verse, which says: "For it came to pass, when the flame went up toward heaven from off the altar, that the angel of the Lord ascended in the flame of the altar." Here, again, we have positive proof that angels are human beings. In this wonderful spiritual manifestation we also have conclusive proof that, so far from condemning Spiritualism, God makes use of it in his dealings with men.

In Zech. i, 8, we read: "I saw by night, and behold a man riding upon a red horse, and he stood among the myrtle-trees that were in the bottom." The tenth verse says: "And the man that stood among the myrtle-trees answered and said, These are they whom the Lord hath sent to walk to and fro through the earth." This answer made known the fact that the man was a messenger, and hence, in the next verse, he is spoken of as such, and is, of course, called an angel. "And they answered the angel of the Lord that stood among the myrtle-trees," etc. You will also notice that this messenger was riding upon a horse. There is nothing strange in this fact, if the messenger was a man. If, however, he was such a being as our modern theologians represent angels to be, he must have appeared quite out of place jogging along on a "red horse," or on a horse of any other color.

In Gal. iv, 14, Paul says: "And my temptation which was in the flesh ye despised not, nor rejected; but received me as an angel of God." He then goes on to approve their manner of receiving him. If he had not been an angel of God, would he have suffered the Gallatians to receive him as one? Or, if angels had been a higher order of beings than men, would he have accepted honors due only to individuals of that higher order? See how promptly, at another time, he put a stop to the proceedings of certain other persons who were about to worship him as a god. Not being a god, he was deeply shocked at the mere thought of receiving honors due only to gods; but, being a messenger or an angel of God, he was pleased to receive the honors due to such a personage. How could you, in Greek, express his official character as messenger of God, without calling him an "angel of God?"

In 2 Sam. xix, 27, we read: "And he hath slandered thy servant unto my lord the king; but my lord the king is an angel of God." This "angel of God" was David, king of Israel. And was not David a human being? If so, are not angels of God human beings? In what respect did Paul and David differ from other angels of God? This is a fair question, and theologians ought to be able to answer it.

In Matt. xviii, 10, we read: "Take heed that ye despise not one of these little ones; for I say unto you, That in heaven their angels do always behold the face of my Father which is in heaven." Dr.

Clarke and many other able Bible critics hold, as do I, that, by this language, Jesus means to assert that every person, and especially every child, has a guardian angel or spirit guide, who has special charge of him and who is admitted into the presence of God to receive instructions concerning his charge. If this be, indeed, what Jesus means to assert, then the assertion fully establishes Spiritualism, for such a guardianship involves the necessity of constant communications between our own world and the world of spirits. If, however, this is not what Jesus means, he is bound to mean that the spirits of the little ones themselves are the angels that "do always behold the face of my father which is in heaven." If this be his meaning, he certainly has human spirits become angels, and thus establishes the doctrine for which I am contending. These two are the only meanings that can possibly be given to the language in question, and either of these meanings, you plainly see, fully establishes Spiritualism.

Thus I might go on and quote hundreds of other passages all going to show that angels are human beings, either in the body or out of it; and that, consequently, all the acts recorded of angels were either the acts of living men or of human spirits. But what need of more proof? I have proved that one office or occupation constitutes one man, or one spirit, an angel, just as another office or occupation constitutes another man, or another spirit, a soldier. The only difference between angels and soldiers consists alone in the difference between their offices or occupations. They are both equally human, and it would be just as easy to establish a separate creation for soldiers as for angels. But why is it, you ask, that there seem to be no females among the angels? And why is it, I ask, that there seem to be no females among the soldiers? The same reason exists in both cases; neither the occupation of the angel, nor that of the soldier, is suitable for females. But many of the angels of the Bible, you say, were spirits. So were many of the soldiers. See Josh. v, 13–15; Dan. x, 20; Rev. xii, 7, and many other places.

If I have not now proved that all angels are human beings, I certainly have proved that some of them are, and that these are exactly like the other angels and fully equal to them in all respects. And does not this amount to a scientific demonstration that all angels are human beings? When a naturalist determines the origin, the general characteristics, etc., of a large number of lions, taken at random as specimens, does he not, at the same time, with absolute certainty determine the origin, the general characteristics, etc., of all other exactly similar lions? And is not this exactly what I have done in regard to all angels? Besides all this, I have proved by Jesus that, whether they ever become angels or not, human spirits certainly do become "as the angels," and "equal unto" them. In proving this I have proved that human spirits can communicate with men and do all other things that can be done by angels. Can you, then, reject Spiritualism without rejecting the Bible?

I will now notice a few of the many cases of spiritual manifestations recorded in the Bible of parties who did not claim to be angels.

In 2 Chron. xviii, 19–21, we read: "And the Lord

said, Who shall entice Ahab, king of Israel, that he may go up and fall at Ramoth-Gilead? And one spake saying after this manner, and another saying after that manner. Then there came out a spirit, and stood before the Lord, and said, I will entice him. And the Lord said unto him, Wherewith? And he said, I will go out and be a lying spirit in the mouth of all his prophets. And the Lord said, Thou shalt entice him, and thou shalt also prevail: go out and do even so." Accordingly, as we learn from the balance of this same chapter, this spirit did go out, and did communicate with Ahab, through certain spiritual mediums, called prophets.

You are bound to admit that this was a genuine spirit; that these prophets were genuine spiritual mediums, and that the communications made through them were genuine spiritual communications. Will you be so kind, then, as to inform us why there may not now be just as genuine spirits, just as genuine spiritual mediums, and just as genuine spiritual communications as there were then? You may attempt to evade this fair and proper question by objecting that the spirit in question was an evil spirit. Such an evasion, however, is no answer. It is only a proof that you are driven to desperation, and that you dare not, on this subject, meet me in fair discussion. Neither the character of the spirit, nor that of the communications made by him, has anything to do with the facts in the case. What we want to know—what all searchers after truth want to know—is: Did the spirit in question, or did he not, actually communicate with Ahab, through certain persons, such as we now call spiritual mediums? If he did, is not the truth of Spiritualism established? If he did not, is not the Bible convicted of falsehood? Which horn of this dilemma will you take?

We would also like to know whether God did, or did not, command the spirit in question to do just what he did. If God did give such a command, was he not commanding the practice of Spiritualism? And if God commanded the practice of Spiritualism, how dare you say, as many of you do, that Spiritualism is of the devil? Does God, think you, in the conducting of his affairs, adopt the practices and the inventions of the devil? Can he not devise means of his own for the conducting of those affairs? If, on the other hand, God did not give the command in question, does not the Bible again stand convicted of falsehood?

Again, admitting that God did give this command, did the spirit in question, or did he not, act wickedly in obeying it? If he did act wickedly, did not God act still more wickedly in giving the command? If you condemn the spirit because he lied, what have you to say of God, by whose command he lied? If, on the other hand, the spirit did not act wickedly, how dare you call him an evil spirit? What do you know of his character, except what you learn from the history of this one affair? Was he not just such a spirit as God wanted? Did not God approve his acts? If he was an evil spirit, how came he to be loafing around God's throne in heaven? Does God keep evil spirits around his throne? Finally, if to get himself out of a similar trouble, God should now command you to lie for him in a similar manner, would you, or would you not, obey that command?

If you would obey it, would you, or would you not, regard your act of obedience as a wicked act, and yourself, in consequence of that act, as a wicked person? If, on the other hand, you would not obey the command, would you not, in so doing, cease to be a Christian? Would you not become a rebel against God? And would you not forfeit all hope of salvation? Think of these things before you condemn that spirit!

You may object further that this affair involved a special miracle—that it was not the spirit, by his own power, that made the communications, but God, who made them through him. Very good. But this makes God himself do the lying. What a wonderful God you will soon have, if you keep on at this rate! So far, however, from this being a special miracle wrought by himself, God did not even know, or, at least, did not seem to know, what the spirit's proposed plans of operation were until he had inquired, and the spirit had informed him. If God himself had already planned this lying campaign, why should he have called on others to propose a plan? And how could the spirit have known upon what plan he was to act, until God had informed him?

From the language of the text, it is evident that the spirit fully understood his own skill in lying and in making communications to men through spiritual mediums, and that he had his plans all fully matured before he offered to God his extremely valuable services. If he had not frequently practiced making communications to men, through spiritual mediums, how could he have so confidently proposed to God to make them, through so many different mediums, on the present occasion? Since he did not ask of God any instructions in regard to the plan of this campaign, or any aid in carrying out that plan, and since God did not offer him either of these things, how dare you assert that he needed, or that he received, either the one or the other? And if he had power of his own to make such communications, what proofs have you that similar spirits, of the present time, have not the same power to make similar communications? Is anything ever annihilated? If not, is not the power by which that spirit acted bound to be still in existence? And does anything exist without a use? If not, are we not bound to conclude that the power of spirits to communicate with men is still being exercised, and that spiritual communications are still being made?

In 2 Kings ii, 15, we read: "And when the sons of the prophets which were to view at Jericho saw him, they said, The spirit of Elijah doth rest on Elisha." This was spoken after Elijah had entered the spirit world. Did his spirit, then, rest upon Elisha, and, through him as a medium, make prophetic communications to men, or does the Bible stand convicted of falsehood?

In Job iv. 14–17, we read: "Fear came upon me, and trembling, which made all my bones to shake. Then a spirit passed before my face; the hair of my flesh stood up: It stood still, but I could not discern the form thereof: an image was before mine eyes, there was silence, and I heard a voice saying, Shall mortal man be more just than God?" Was the patient, the dignified, the eloquent old Job really a spiritual medium, and did he actually see a spirit, and hear it speak, as he says he did, or is his whole account of the affair an outrageous falsehood? If he actually saw a spirit, and heard it speak, was not Spiritualism, in his day, an established fact? And was not Spiritualism, in this case, practiced by a good man and a good spirit? Are you certain, then, that you do not lie when you so confidently assert that Spiritualism is of the devil? Were Job and the good spirit in question serving the devil?

In 1 Sam. xxviii we learn that the spirit of Samuel appeared to a noted spiritual medium at Endor, and, through her, made some remarkable spiritual communications to Saul, king of Israel. Those who claim to be orthodox Christians call this medium a "witch," a "hag," etc., and often embellish their Bibles and other religious books with vile pictures of her—pictures which, in their vileness, are true reflections of the persons in whose imaginations they are conceived. These zealous Christians take it for granted that the fact of this woman's communing with the spirit of Samuel, a man of God, was utterly damning, both to her character and to her beauty. The Bible, however, does not say a word against either her character or her beauty. It does not even intimate that she ever called up evil spirits or did anything else inconsistent with the character of a good and beautiful woman. Indeed, so far from calling her, as you do, by the foul nicknames, "witch," "hag," etc., the Bible describes her as a kind and noble-hearted woman. See the last five verses of this same chapter. We have nothing to do, however, with either her private character or her beauty. The only question with which we have to deal is, Did she, or did she not, call up the spirit of Samuel, or of any other person, and, from him, receive spiritual communications? The Bible says she did. What do you say? If she did actually receive spiritual communications, was not Spiritualism, in her day, an established fact? And was the spirit of Samuel an evil spirit?

You will probably resort, as usual, to the special miracle evasion, and claim that God, on that particular occasion, gave this woman power to do that which, at other times, she could not have done. So far from this being the case, however, her reputation for doing such things was well established before this event occurred. Indeed, it was her fame for skill in such things that induced Saul to consult her; and, so far from having anything to do in the affair, God was not, at that time, on speaking terms with Saul. Besides this, if the woman had not well known her ability to call up spirits, would she so promptly and so confidently have undertaken to call up whomsoever Saul should name? Could she have known that, through her, God was about to perform a special miracle? Would you so confidently undertake to call up a spirit, believing, at the same time, that you could not do any such thing? So far from claiming this as a special miracle, the Bible describes it simply as an ordinary historical event, and you have no right to claim as a miracle an event for which the Bible sets up no such claim.

In Lev. xx, 27, we read: "A man also or a woman that hath a familiar spirit, or that is a wizard, shall surely be put to death." In Deut. xviii, 10, 11, we read: "There shall not be found among you a charmer, or a consulter with familiar spirits. . . ." In 2 Kings xxi, 6, we learn that Manasseh "dealt with familiar spirits and wizards." You will notice that Manasseh is charged, not with attempting, or with pretending, to deal with familiar spirits, but with actually dealing with them. In the sixth verse of the next chapter we read: "And the soul that turneth after such as have familiar spirits, and after wizards, to go a whoring after them, I will even set my face against that soul, and will cut him off from among his people." These passages, and scores more like them, all go to prove that, among the Hebrews, men actually could, and actually did, consult with spirits. Spiritualism, then, was an established fact.

The last passage quoted shows plainly enough, too, that it was the abuse, and not the proper use, of Spiritualism that God condemned. The Hebrews, having always lived among an idolatrous people, were themselves extremely prone to idolatry. Many of them, therefore, went "a whoring" after familiar spirits, wizards, etc.; that is, they idolatrously offered to these beings that worship which was due to God alone. Against those who practiced this form of idolatry the penalty of death was pronounced, and was, on many occasions, actually inflicted.

The laws against consulting with familiar spirits were given by God himself, and were directed, not against those who tried, or who pretended, to consult with these spirits, but against those who actually did consult with them. When God gave these laws, did he, or did he not, believe that spirits could be called up, without his aid, and consulted? Would he have enacted laws against things which he did not believe could be done? And if he believed that spirits could be called up and consulted, must not Spiritualism have been a fact? Could God have been deceived in regard to these things? Under the laws in question, many persons were found guilty, and were put to death. And would God, think you, have had persons executed for things which he knew that they could not do, and that they had not done?

In the Endor affair, which I have just noticed, you claimed that spirits could be called up and consulted only by the miraculous interposition of God's own power. If this claim be correct, then God had very severe laws enacted against the exercise of his own miraculous power. He also had vast numbers of innocent persons put to death, as criminals, in the most cruel manner, either for crimes which had never been committed at all, or for those which he himself had committed. In your mad war against Spiritualism, what kind of a being are you making of your God? And what kind of a being are you also making of Jesus? In the New Testament we learn that he and his disciples were almost daily engaged in casting out evil spirits. But, if spirits can be called up only by the interposition of God's miraculous power, how came those evil spirits in the men from whom Jesus and his disciples expelled them? Did God call up those spirits and put them into men? If not, did Jesus, exercising God's almighty power, call them up? Of necessity, he must have done so, and all this simply that he might afflict men who had never injured him, and that he and his disciples might gain applause by casting out poor spirits, who never would have been in those men, had they not been called up and placed there by Jesus himself.

With such facts as these before you, dare you longer deny that Spiritualism, just as we now teach it, did exist among God's chosen people? Dare you longer deny that spirits were frequently called up and consulted, without the interposition of God's miraculous power? Dare you assert that what was possible among the Jews, is impossible among us? Dare you assert that what occurred so frequently among the Jews, never occurs at all among us? Dare you assert that what was of God among the Jews, is of the devil among us? If, since the times of which we are speaking, any barrier has been erected, to cut off all communication between our world and the world of spirits, will you be so kind as to inform us when that barrier was erected, where it was erected, why it was erected, how it was erected, and by whom it was erected? Will you also be so kind as to inform us how new-born spirits from earth manage to pass that barrier, on their way to heaven, when the passage is totally impracticable to older and more experienced spirits?

In Matt. xvii we read of four noted spiritual mediums, Jesus, Peter, James, and John, who called up, and conversed with, the spirits of two equally noted men, Moses and Elias. You dare not deny that this event actually occurred. You may claim, however, that this was a special miracle, performed by the divine power of Jesus, and that men could never have thus called up and conversed with spirits. But have I not already proved that men did frequently thus call up spirits and consult with them? Have I not also proved that to charge God with all that was ever done of this kind of work, would be to charge him with the horrible act of having multitudes of innocent persons put to death for crimes which he himself had committed? Dare you bring against God so horribly blasphemous an accusation? Besides this, what does Jesus himself say on the subject? "Verily, verily, I say unto you, he that believeth on me, the works that I do shall he do also; and greater works than these shall he do" (John xiv, 12). Calling up spirits, and conversing with them, was one of the most important works that Jesus did, and power to do this, and even greater works than this, he promises to those that believe on him. And are there, at the present time, any that believe on him? If there are, and if Jesus was not an impostor, are not those persons bound to possess, according to his promise, the power to call up spirits, and to perform all the other works that Jesus himself was wont to perform? Deny this, if you dare!

In Mark xvi, 17, 18, Jesus says: "And these signs shall follow them that believe: In my name shall they cast out devils; they shall speak with new new tongues . . . they shall lay hands on the sick and they shall recover." This was spoken in the last meeting that Jesus held with his disciples on earth. In Matt. x, 8, Jesus gives his disciples the following commands: "Heal the sick, cleanse the lepers, raise the dead, cast out devils: freely ye have received, freely give." In the last two verses of Matthew Jesus, in his final instructions to his disciples, recalls to their minds these commands, and all the others that he had ever given them, then instructs them to teach all nations to observe these things, and, finally, to encourage them in the discharge of all these duties, says: "And lo, I am with you alway, even unto the end of the world."

From the last clause quoted, it is evident that the duties which were assigned to the disciples were assigned to them, not in their individual capacity, to cease at their death, but in their official, or representative, capacity, to continue, through their successors, "alway, even unto the end of the world." The same is also true of the signs that were to follow them that believe. Indeed, upon the ability to successfully perform the duties of healing the sick, casting out devils, raising the dead, etc., were to depend most of the signs that were to follow them that believe. Those duties, then, were assigned to all nations, and for all time. The signs, too—the successful accomplishment of these duties—were to fellow all of those that believe, of all nations, during all time, "even unto the end of the world."

From all this, it is evident that the duties of healing the sick, casting out devils, raising the dead, etc., are still just as binding upon "all nations" as they were at the first, upon the apostles themselves. The signs, too, which were to accompany these duties, or, rather, which were to consist in the ability to perform them, are all just as fully promised to those of the present time who believe on Jesus, as they were to the apostles themselves. The duties of healing the sick, etc., constituting, as they certainly did, the principal portion of the gospel which was commanded to be preached, were certainly intended to be as permanent as the gospel of which they thus constituted so essential a part. If, then, it be still a duty to preach the gospel, it is certainly a duty to preach all those things which constitute the gospel. So of the signs in question; they were to be inseparable from belief on Jesus. If, then, belief on Jesus is to continue "alway, even unto the end of the world," so are these signs also, which were to accompany that belief, to continue for the same period.

Since Jesus never imposed as a duty, upon his followers, anything impossible for them to perform, we may be sure that the duties of healing the sick, casting out devils, raising the dead, etc., were then, and are now, possible to "all nations," who were to be taught to observe these and all the other duties which Jesus had ever commanded his disciples to observe. But, in order that the duty of healing the sick might always remain possible, it was necessary that sickness should always remain among men. If there were no sick to be healed, it would be impossible to heal the sick. So of casting out devils. The performance of this duty would be impossible if there were no devils to be cast out. This duty being, as I have already shown, a permanent one, imposed on the followers of Jesus for all time, the existence of devils among men is bound to be equally permanent. But who and what are these devils? Simply evil spirits—the spirits of bad men—spirits that get control of many mediumistic persons, and use that control for evil purposes. All that I said of angels applies to these spirits, who are simply bad angels. To cast out these evil spirits, that is, to break up their improper control, is as much a duty now as it ever was; and, to those who believe on Jesus, the performance of this duty is just as easy as it ever was. No man, be his pretensions what they may, who is either unwilling or unable to perform this duty, can justly claim to be a true believer on Jesus.

And the raising of the dead, you ask, was this, too, imposed upon the followers of Jesus as a permanent duty? It certainly was. And can this duty still be performed? With the utmost ease, by those who believe on Jesus. The performance of this duty is of almost daily occurrence in all countries, and all communities. This is especially the case among Spiritualists. Whenever they call up a spirit, they raise the dead; and this is all the form of raising the dead that was ever enjoined, as a duty, upon the apostles or upon any others. To suppose, as most of you do, that, by the raising of the dead, we are to understand the revivifying of the bodies of the dead, is a great error. We are not required to raise the bodies of the dead, but to raise the dead themselves. Their bodies are merely their old habitations. In raising the dead we rarely have anything to do with these old habitations. Indeed, the body of a man, when once forsaken, is very rarely fit to be reinhabited, and when it is fit, it is rarely possible to restart to running the physical machinery of life. Since, then, the raising of the dead, in this manner, is so rarely possible, it could not have been enjoined upon all as a duty, nor could it have been promised as one of the signs that should certainly "follow them that believe." As I have already shown, however, the command to raise the dead, and the power to do so, are plainly given to every one "that believeth." The command, then, can mean nothing more nor less than the raising of the dead in their spiritual forms, as we Spiritualists are wont to raise them, for the purpose of consulting with them upon all subjects of interest to ourselves and to the world. In commanding us to raise the dead, in this manner, Jesus simply repealed, as he had both the power and the right to repeal, the law by which the Jews, on account of their idolatrous tendencies, had been forbidden to thus raise the dead. Jesus never violated the laws of his country, nor taught his followers to violate them; and yet, in raising the dead—the spirits of Moses and Elias—in the manner of which I am speaking, he would have been guilty of a capital offense against the laws of his country, had the law against thus raising the dead been still in force. By thus repealing the law in question, Jesus brought men into full communion with the spirit-world, and made Spiritualism an essential element in Christianity.

That my views are correct in regard to what Jesus meant by the raising of the dead, in the passages to which I have referred, is still further proved by a dialogue which took place between Abraham and a certain rich man who, it seems, had had the misfortune to be sent to hell. In the course of this dialogue, which we find recorded in Luke xvi, 19–31, the rich man says: "I pray thee, therefore, father, that thou wouldst send him [Lazarus] to my father's house: for I have five brethren; that he may testify unto them, lest they also come into this place of torment. Abraham saith unto him, They have Moses and the prophets; let them hear them. And he said, Nay, father Abraham: but if one went unto them from the dead, they will repent. And he said unto him, If they hear not Moses and the prophets, neither will they be persuaded though one rose from the dead."

I suppose that no one will claim that the dead body of Lazarus, which, even before death, was putrid with sores, was ever carried to Abraham's bosom. If, then, Lazarus had been sent back to earth, to the rich man's brethren, he would certainly have gone in his spiritual form, and his communications would certainly have been genuine spiritual communications; and yet this would have been what both the rich man and Abraham designated an arising from the dead. Both Abraham and the rich man seemed to regard this mode of arising from the dead as something that could take place at any time. Abraham refused to have Lazarus thus arise from the dead, not because such an arising was impossible or improper, but simply because he regarded as utterly useless, if not improper, the errand on which the rich man wished Lazarus sent. And, under the circumstances that surrounded them—being themselves both inhabitants of the realms of the dead—were not Abraham and the rich man both competent authorities in regard to what constitutes an arising from the dead? Jesus seems to think that they were.

If, however, you still insist that, in commanding his disciples, and, through them, all nations, to raise the dead, Jesus meant for them to revivify the dead bodies of deceased men, what do you gain thereby, and what do you cause me to lose? When the apostles and others raised the dead in this way, if, indeed, they ever did so, did they not, of necessity, call back the spirits of the dead from their new abodes in the world of spirits? And if the apostles and other spiritual mediums could thus call back spirits for the purpose of having them re-enter their old tenements of clay, could not the same mediums just as easily call back the same spirits for any other purpose? Was the presence of a dead body of any service either to the medium in calling the spirit back, or to the spirit in coming back? Do you not perceive, then, that the raising of the dead in this form, as in all others, is a positive proof of the truth of Spiritualism?

You object, however, that, even among the most aristocratic churches of the present time, none of those spiritual powers are to be found which Jesus promised to "them that believe." Very well. This simply proves that your most aristocratic churches are not composed of "them that believe." These churches are all man-made, pride-engendering, fashion-fostering institutions. They have nothing in common with Jesus. He did not know them. His promises were to "them that believe," and these are never to be found in those grand resorts of fashion and pride, your modern churches. You would better remonstrate with Jesus for thus neglecting your churches, and bestowing his spiritual gifts upon "them that believe"—upon the despised Spiritualists. Say to him: "My dear Jesus, such conduct will never do! It will injure your popularity among the wealthy classes! It will go to prove that the despised Spiritualists are your true believers, since they seem to be the only ones who possess the spiritual gifts which you promised to "them that believe." This condition of affairs cannot be permitted to continue; therefore, reform, Jesus, reform! and come into our church!"

In 1 John iv, 1-3, we read: "Beloved, believe not every spirit, but try the spirits whether they are of God . . . Every spirit that confesseth that Jesus Christ is come in the flesh is of God: and every spirit that confesseth not that Jesus Christ is come in the flesh is not of God." These instructions to "try the spirits" were given to men here on earth. But, in order to "try these spirits," according to these instructions, is it not absolutely necessary that the spirits be also here on earth, where we are, and that they communicate to us their opinions in regard to Jesus Christ? And if this is not Spiritualism, what is it? Better caution John to be a little more prudent in his language. Have him at least refrain from declaring that some of these communicating spirits are "of God." Have him denounce the whole thing as "of the devil."

Paul devotes the entire twelfth chapter of 1 Cor. to a description of the various gifts that were to be possessed by the true followers of Jesus. Among these gifts he specifies those of healing diseases, of prophesying, of speaking in divers tongues, of performing miracles, of discerning spirits—of doing all those things which Spiritualists do, or, at least, profess to do, at the present time. And these gifts were not to be the transient possessions of the believers of that age alone, but, as I have already shown, were to "follow them that believe," "alway, even unto the end of the world." Should not Paul be reproved for thus confirming the truths of Spiritualism?

From John's instructions to "try the spirits

whether they are of God," etc., we learn that some of them "are of God," and that these communicate with men, confessing "that Jesus Christ is come in the flesh." How dare you, then, assert that all spiritual manifestations are of the devil? Nearly all of you do this whenever you are forced to admit the genuineness of the manifestations themselves. In doing this, however, you are simply doing what your models, the bigoted Jews, did in regard to similar manifestations produced through the mediumship of Jesus himself. "He hath a devil and is mad; why hear ye him?" "This fellow doth not cast out devils, but by Beelzebub, the prince of devils." These and similar expressions were constantly being hurled at Jesus, because of the wonderful exhibitions of his mediumistic powers. And in your cruel war against Spiritualism, what have you thus far done but use the very same language which the orthodox churchmen of his time used against his spiritualism?

When Jesus approached them, walking on the water, his disciples at once believed it to be a spirit. Could they have believed this unless they had been believers in Spiritualism? In his comments on this passage, Dr. Clarke says: "That the spirits of the dead might and did appear, was a doctrine held by the greatest and holiest men that ever existed; and a doctrine which the cavillers, free-thinkers and bound-thinkers, of different ages have never been able to disprove." And are you prepared to condemn "the greatest and the holiest men that ever existed?" If you are, then I would rather fall with them than stand with you.

When Peter stood rapping on the door of the

house in which the disciples and others were holding a prayer-meeting, they at once believed it to be a spirit rapping—Peter's spirit, come to them as an angel from the prison, in which they knew he had been confined, and in which they, naturally enough, supposed he had been put to death. Dr. Clarke and many other able writers concur in this view. If the disciples had not been believers in Spiritualism, could they have thus believed that it was a spirit whose rappings they heard, and whose form was visible at the door? In other words, could they have believed that these were phenomena in the existence of which they, at the same time, did not believe? When they believed that a spirit was at that very moment rapping on their door, were they, or were they not, believers in spirit rappings? Are you not bound to admit that they were as thorough believers in Spiritualism as are any of us at the present day?

You will doubtless object, however, that, in this instance, it was not a spirit that appeared and that produced the rappings upon the door. Very well. This is so much the better for my argument. I did not introduce this case to prove that a spirit did appear, but to prove that the apostles were firm believers in the phenomena of Spiritualism. Had they been unbelievers in these phenomena, they would not have been expecting any such phenomena, and would certainly have been greatly astonished if a spirit had made its appearance and had rapped upon their door. As it was, however, the case was exactly the opposite of this. They were astonished, not because it was, but because it was not a spirit that made its appearance and rapped upon their door. Had it proved to be a spirit, as their faith in such phenomena easily led them to believe that it was, they would not have been in the least astonished. They were doubtless accustomed to spiritual manifestations, especially at their seances or prayer meetings, and were evidently expecting some such manifestations on the present occasion. Hence, when Peter made his appearance, in the manner described, they all, at once, believed it to be that which, more than anything else, they were expecting. They believed it to be a spirit, coming to them as an "angel," or messenger, and making known its arrival, as they evidently were expecting it would, by rappings upon the door or upon some other object. So much more probable did they believe it to be that a spirit would make its appearance, in the manner described, than that Peter, in the body, should thus make his appearance, that they could hardly be made to believe that it was indeed he, and not an "angel," or spirit messenger.

With all these plain facts before you, dare you longer deny that the apostles were firm believers in those spiritual phenomena upon which Spiritualism is founded? And can you condemn Spiritualists, on account of their belief, without condemning the apostles for holding the same belief? If the belief of the apostles in Spiritualism was founded in either ignorance or error, can you show any good reason why the same may not be equally true of all the other doctrines in which they believed, and in which you follow them? Have we not their authority as fully for Spiritualism as you have it for any of your doctrines? And is not that authority worth as much in our case as it is in yours? Shall we accept it, then, in both cases, or reject it in both? We cannot accept it in the one case, and reject it in the other.

Were it necessary to do so, I could still go on indefinitely, and, from the Bible, pile up proof upon proof of the truth of Spiritualism, and of its acceptability in the sight of heaven. More proof, however, is unnecessary. I will, therefore, briefly recapitulate my arguments, and then close.

1. I have proved that Spiritualism, substantially as we now teach it, prevailed throughout the entire period covered by Biblical history.

2. I have proved that angels are human beings, and that all the transactions of angelic spirits with men are phenomena pertaining to Spiritualism.

3. I have proved that spirits, whether they ever become angels or not, certainly do become as the angels, and equal unto them. In proving this, I have proved that human spirits have power to appear unto men, to communicate with them, and to do all other things that can be done by angels.

4. I have proved that Abraham, Jacob, Job, Manoah, and many others of the greatest and best men of the Bible were Spiritualists and good mediums.

5. I have proved that God approved Spiritualism, in its legitimate uses, and that he often had men practice it.

6. I have proved that Jesus and the apostles were all Spiritualists and good mediums; that they promised that these Spiritual phenomena, as signs, should follow the true believers in Christianity, "alway, even unto the end of the world," and that they imposed upon their followers, of all nations and of

all ages, certain duties which cannot possibly be performed except through the instrumentality of Spiritualism.

7. I have proved that, if you deny my arguments, you make God a liar, and make him have multitudes of innocent persons put to death for crimes committed by himself.

8. I have proved that Spiritualism rests upon the same authority as do the fundamental doctrines of the Christian religion, and that if this authority be worthless in the one case, it is bound to be equally worthless in the other.

9. Finally, I have proved that, in order to overthrow Spiritualism, you must prove that the Bible is false, and that Jesus and the apostles were liars. What more proof do you want?

LECTURE II.

SPIRITUALISM SUSTAINED BY THE CHRISTIAN CHURCH.

In proving the truths of Spiritualism, by the Bible, as I did in my last lecture, I addressed my arguments to those persons only who profess to have full faith in the truth of all the teachings of that book. To these persons I did not consider any defense of the Bible necessary; and, with my present views of the Bible, I could not consistently have made any defense of it, even had I considered a defense necessary. Regarding myself as counsel for Spiritualism in the suit brought against it in the great court of the world, by the Christian priesthood of the present time and their followers, and preferring to win the cause of my client on the exclusive testimony of the plaintiff's witnesses, I simply regarded the Bible as their most important witness, and, in the cross-examination, I elicited testimony so damaging to their cause that they will be compelled either to abandon the suit or to impeach the testimony of this their principal witness. So, in my present lecture, I shall treat the Christian Church as one of the plaintiff's principal witnesses. I shall accept as truth all that this unwilling witness testifies in favor of Spiritualism, and shall thus, as in the case of the Bible, throw the burden of denial on the plaintiffs themselves. And, whether they admit or deny the testimony of this witness and that of their former witness, the Bible, their case is hopelessly lost.

The doings and the teachings of Jesus and his disciples are the last things recorded in Biblical history, and the first things recorded in the history of the Christian Church. These persons, therefore, belong both to Biblical and to post-Biblical times. Their testimony, then, is of the highest importance, whether we regard them as noted men of the Bible, or as the founders of the Christian Church. In my last lecture I had them, as characters of the Bible, give the most positive testimony in support of the truth of Spiritualism. I will now recall them to the witness-stand, and have them, as the highest authorities of the Christian Church, continue their testimony so damaging to the cause of the opposers of Spiritualism.

In Heb. i, 14, Paul, in speaking of angels, says: "Are they not all ministering spirits, sent forth to minister for them who shall be heirs of salvation?" From this we learn that all the angels are ministering spirits—that is, spirits employed as ministers or messengers. With equal truth it might also be said that all ministering spirits are angels. In my last lecture I proved that the term angel means nothing more nor less than messenger, or ministering spirit. I proved that it is office or occupation, and that alone, which constitutes a man an angel, just as it is office or occupation, and that alone, which constitutes a man a soldier, a magistrate, or a manufacturer. No one, therefore, be his origin and nature what they may, can be an angel, unless he be occupied, in some way, as a messenger or a minister; and, conversely, no one, be his origin and nature what they may, can be thus occupied without becoming, during the continuance of that occupation, an angel. From this, it is clear that an angel ceases to exist as such the moment the office expires, or the occupation ceases, which constituted him an angel, just as a soldier, a magistrate, or a manufacturer ceases to exist as such the moment he retires from the office, or the occupation, that constituted him such. An angel could no more exist as such, without employment to constitute him such, than a current of water could exist as such without motion to constitute it a current. As the loss of motion destroys a current as such, and reduces it to mere water, so the loss of employment destroys an angel as such, and reduces him to a mere man, or to an ordinary spirit. From this it is clear that an individual may be a mere man, or an ordinary spirit, to-day, and an angel to-morrow; or an angel to-day, and a mere man, or an ordinary spirit, to-morrow. The whole matter depends upon how he may be employed.

In my last lecture I proved that many, if not all, of the angels who exist in the form of spirits are neither more nor less than human beings who have laid aside the mortal form. Since, then, this entire class of angels are "all ministering spirits, sent forth to minister for them who shall be heirs of salvation," these human spirits are bound to be among those thus "sent forth." How else, indeed, could human spirits be—as Jesus declares that they are—" as the angels which are in heaven," and "equal unto them?"

But why is it, you ask, that you receive no spiritual manifestations, or angelic ministrations, of any kind?

Simply because you are not one of those to whom these things were promised. What right have you to expect any such things? These spiritual ministrations were promised only to "them that believe," and to "them who shall be heirs of salvation." You belong to a very different class of persons. You deny the very signs by which, alone, the divinity of Jesus can be established—the very signs by which, alone, his presence among the people can be made known. In thus denying that these signs do follow "them that believe," you make liars of Jesus and the apostles, who promised these signs to all true believers. In thus denying the only proofs there ever were of the divinity of Jesus, you reduce him to the unenviable condition of an impostor. In this way you accomplish more than has ever been accomplished by the boldest of Infidels.

No matter, then, how prominent you may be as members of fashionable orthodox churches—no matter how long may be your faces, your coat-tails, or your prayers—no matter how loud may be your denunciations of those who reject your dogmas—you are not of "them that believe," and, hence, cannot be of "them who shall be heirs of salvation." And can you expect to enjoy spiritual gifts and spiritual ministrations in the existence of which you do not believe? Is it not evident that you are of that class to whom, on account of their unbelief, Jesus promised damnation? And would it not be well for you to ascertain just what damnation is, and commence preparing for it?

In Heb. xi Paul recounts a long list of patriarchs, prophets, martyrs, and other worthies, who had departed this life, from the righteous Abel down to those who had died in his own time; then, referring to all these departed persons—these spirits—in a body, he opens the next chapter as follows: "Wherefore, seeing we also are compassed about with so great a cloud of witnesses, let us lay aside every weight, and the sin which doth so easily beset us, and let us run with patience the race that is set before us."

Since the persons to whom Paul here refers had all passed through the change called death, they were certainly all spirits at the time the great apostle used this language. If Paul tells the truth, then human spirits, in his time, did, like a great cloud, compass about men still in the body, and did witness all their actions. And is not this a positive proof of the truth of Spiritualism in one of its grand, its glorious, its heaven-attested and heaven-approved phases?

To render this proof still stronger Paul proceeds, farther on in the same chapter, to enumerate several material objects, such as mountains, fire, trumpets, etc., and declares that unto these things "ye are not come." Then, in contrast with these material objects, he continues: "But ye are come unto Mount Sion, and unto the city of the living God, the heavenly Jerusalem, and to an innumerable company of angels, to the general assembly and church of the first-born, which are written in heaven, and to God the Judge of all, and to the spirits of just men made perfect, and to Jesus the mediator of the new covenant . . ."

Paul does not predict that, after death, ye shall come unto all these things, in some far away and indefinite place, but historically declares that now and here, "ye are come unto" them. Where, then, were those spirits, those angels, etc., bound to be in order to be thus "come unto" by men still on earth and still in the body? Were not those spirits, etc., bound to be also here on earth? Could men have thus "come unto" them, if they had been, where you now place them, far away from earth, in some unknown direction, and in some undiscoverable portion of infinite space? And how could that "innumerable company of angels," and of "the spirits of just men made perfect," have "compassed about" those men, like "so great a cloud of witnesses," without being present where those men were?

Paul speaks of the presence of "angels," and of "the spirits of just men made perfect," of "so great a cloud of witnesses," as a fact fully accepted by the Hebrews, whom he urges, on account of the presence of such witnesses, to cultivate purity of heart and of life. Unless, then, you can prove that Paul taught, and that the Hebrews believed, a monstrous lie, you are bound to admit that, in those days, "the spirits of just men made perfect" were present, as witnesses, round about men still in the body. And where are those spirits now? Have they, since Paul's time, been banished from earth? If not, are they not still present, like a great cloud, witnessing the actions of men? If they have been banished, will you be so kind as to inform us when they were banished, why they were banished, how their banishment was carried into effect, and in what particular portion of infinite space they now are? If you cannot give us this information, does not Spiritualism stand fully established and fully approved? Can you, without the aid of Spiritualism, prove that there is any spirit world at all, or that man has any conscious existence beyond the change called death?

What ideas of heaven and of hell do you now teach that were not borrowed from the ancient pagans? Those pagans taught that the earth was stationary in the center of the universe, and that what we call the sky was a solid structure or firmament placed, like a hollow sphere, around the earth, or, rather, like an inverted bowl, over the earth. On the upper or convex side of this inverted bowl they located the home of their gods, and of their departed heroes and other great men. And do you not teach this same pagan heaven to-day? What other heaven have you? And what are you but pagans?

To those pagans *up* meant a definite and unchangeable direction. To them it was clear that two persons, starting up from the same point, the one at noon, the other at midnight, would travel in the same direction, and on the same straight line, and would reach the firmament, or inverted bowl, at the same point. Those pagans, then, very consistently placed their heaven on the upper side of this firmament. At any rate, it was perfectly safe to place heaven up there, since no one, in those times, was able to prove that it was not there. Modern science, however, has now entirely dissipated the firmament or solid sky on which that heaven was located; and the disappearance of that firmament necessitated the disappearance of the heaven that rested upon it. In other words, it is now fully demonstrated that no such firmament, no such heaven, ever existed at all. And yet this utterly dissipated heaven of the benighted old pagans is the only heaven of the orthodox Christians of to-day. If your heaven be not now, as of old, stationary above a stationary earth—above the firmament—the immovable blue sky, where is it, and what is it? Dare you even attempt to answer these fair questions?

Because you can do no better, you still teach that heaven, the dwelling-place of God, of angels, and of " the spirits of just men made perfect," is up; and this vague teaching satisfies the ignorant and unthinking masses among us, just as it satisfied the same class of persons among the ancient pagans. Intelligent persons, however, cannot thus be satisfied, and every minister of the gospel, who has sufficient intelligence to be successful in his profession, knows very well that, in teaching this vague doctrine, he is binding upon the minds of the people a remnant of old pagan mythology, founded in an utter ignorance of the true structure of the universe. Ministers of this class are true shepherds. They feed their sheep upon the mythological stuff which I have been describing, simply because the sheep like it, and because, while feeding upon it, they make the finest yield to the shepherds, of wool and of mutton. These intelligent shepherds have an eye only to the profits. They themselves never think of swallowing a morsel of the stuff upon which they feed their sheep. A minister of the gospel who is sufficiently ignorant— and there are many such—to believe what he preaches, is far too ignorant to ever become eminently successful in his profession. Such a minister is like a real shepherd who would undertake to eat real fodder with his real sheep—he is a failure.

Intelligent ministers of the gospel take no stock themselves in the mythological heaven which they preach. Like all other skilful manipulators of worthless stock, they sell all the shares they can, and at as high figures as they can, but they never invest their own money in any such stock. For the benefit of the ignorant, upon whom they chiefly depend for their converts and their salaries, they still teach, as I have already stated, that heaven is up in what is called the sky. In other words, they still teach the old mythological heaven of the pagans, without any change except in regard to the number of gods said to dwell up there.

But what does *up* mean? Simply outward from the center of the earth, indefinitely, in all directions. Up is only a relative term. Up, to one man or one locality, may be down to another man or another locality. Up, at one hour of the day, may be, and actually is, down at another hour of the day. Your spirits, then, starting out, at the same moment, from different points on the earth's surface, or at different moments, from the same point, and going upward to find heaven, would depart from the earth in different directions, and on constantly diverging lines. Traveling thus, with the speed of light, through all the ages of eternity, no two of them would ever meet, and no one of them would ever find your fabled heaven.

Through our great telescopes we now look forth in all directions to regions so distant that light, passing from them to the earth, reaches it only after a journey of a hundred thousand years. Scattered throughout this whole immeasurable expanse, we find worlds without number, all having physical constitutions and physical laws similar to those of our own world. Nowhere do we find a spot better fitted to be a heaven to the inhabitants of the earth than is earth herself. Space is everywhere the same. The firmament—the great inverted blue bowl, upon which the mythological heaven of the pagans and of the Christians rested—is found to have no existence. The blue is merely the color of the atmosphere which surrounds us, and does not exist except near the earth's surface. The sun, the moon, and the stars, which, to keep them from falling down upon the earth, both pagans and Christians had "set," or stuck, like nails, into the under side of their firmament, are found to be freely revolving in space. Every vestige of your heaven disappears.

From all this it is evident that earth herself must afford all the heaven there is for us, earth's children. Indeed, heaven, of necessity, consists in condition, and not in location. On any other hypothesis you find yourselves involved in difficulties and absurdities from which no amount of sophistry will ever enable you to extricate yourselves. Why, then, persist in the worse than pagan attempt to locate your heaven at a distance from earth, far out in space, you know not where? Why continue to banish the spirits of the righteous afar from those they love, near whom they would like to remain, and to whom, by their angelic ministrations, they might do much good? Is distance from earth essential to happiness? If it is, does the happiness increase directly as the distance, or as the square of the distance? Give me the rule, and tell me exactly how far your heaven is from earth, and I will tell you exactly how many times happier you would be there than you would be on the top of Mount Washington. Indeed, I could even tell you how much happier you would be in the garret of an eight-story building than you would be on the first floor.

Do any of you really believe that God actually does thus carry away and imprison the spirits of the righteous? Do you really believe that he actually does prevent even the pious mother from revisiting her darling babes, and shielding them, by her angelic presence, from the evil influences of the legions of devils whom your priests blasphemously charge him with having deliberately made and turned loose to ruin mankind? Could any place, however distant it might be from earth, ever be a heaven to such a mother, while she knew that devils were in her old home, leading her poor, dear children down to the unutterable torments of a never-ending hell? If not permitted, at such times, to go to her children, would not your heaven become to her a place of intolerable torment? And what kind of a being do you make of your God by these your blasphemous teachings?

How much more beautiful than all this, how much more glorious, how much more honorable to God, are the teachings of Spiritualism, which have us, while yet in the body, "compassed about with so great a cloud of witnesses," with "an innumerable company of angels," and with "the spirits of just men made perfect!" And what could more powerfully influence men to purity of thought and of life than the known presence of such glorified beings? Many of these were once the idols of our own loving hearts, the lights of our own happy homes. Our parents, our brothers, our sisters, our children, glorified beyond the power of words to express, but none the less dear, they come to us now in their robes of snow—on their wings of light. "Compassed about with so great a cloud of witnesses," we can do no wicked act, indulge in no wicked thought. The sorrows of earth are forgotten, joy unspeakable thrills our bosoms, and we long to become like the loved, the beautiful, the glorified beings around us. Oh! how great an incentive to purity of heart and of life—how great a source of joy unutterable—is lost to you by your mad rejection of these beautiful teachings of the Bible and of Spiritualism!

In Matt. xxvii, 52, 53, we read: "And the graves were opened, and many bodies of the saints which slept arose, and came out of the graves after his resurrection, and went into the holy city, and appeared unto many." Now turning to 1 Cor. xv, 42-44, we learn from Paul the nature of the body with which a saint arises: 'It is sown in corruption, it is raised in incorruption; it is sown in dishonor, it is raised in glory; it is sown in weakness, it is raised in power; it is sown a natural body, it is raised a spiritual body. There is a natural body, and there is a spiritual body." In the thirty-fifth verse we read: "But some man will say, How are the dead raised up? and with what body do they come?" From this we learn that the raising up of the dead, and their coming with bodies, are events, not of the future, but of the present time. The question is not how will the dead be raised up at some far distant and indefinite period of the future, and with what bodies will they come? but how are they raised up now, and with what bodies do they now come?

Paul proceeds to answer these questions at length, and together with much more, all tending to convey the same ideas, uses the language which I first quoted. In all that he says upon the subject he speaks of the sowing of the natural body, and of the raising up of the spiritual body, as of events both of which occur equally in the present time. As the new grain, by a law of its being, is quickened, and caused to proceed from the old grain when the latter dies, and as an immediate consequence of its dying, so, as Paul beautifully explains, the new, or spiritual body, by a similar law of its being, is quickened, in like manner, and caused to proceed from the old body, when the latter dies, and as an immediate consequence of its dying. With equal propriety the great apostle might have continued this wonderfully beautiful comparison by saying that, as the new grain, when once quickened and separated from the old, never again needs that old and lifeless grain, and never again returns to it; so the new—the spiritual—body, when once quickened and separated from the old, never again needs that old and lifeless body, and never again returns to reinhabit it. When once dead, both the old grain and the old body are resolved into their original elements, which are then free to enter into new combinations—into the forms of plants, of animals, etc.

From all this it is clear that those saints "which arose, . . . went into the holy city, and appeared unto many" were simply spirits in such bodies as spirits possess. Indeed, with any other than spiritual bodies, they could not have been "as the angels which are in heaven," as Jesus declares that saints are in the resurrection. The bodies of those saints were not the gross material bodies which they had once inhabited. Those bodies had returned to dust, and the dust, or portions of it, at least, had probably entered into the composition of other human bodies. There is no authentic record of any instance in which a human body, after undergoing decomposition, has ever been recomposed, or reinhabited; and the Bible does not even intimate that any such event will ever occur. Such a recomposition, indeed, would be simply a new creation, which could just as easily be performed upon matter which had never, as yet, entered into the composition of a human body.

Notwithstanding all these indisputable facts, however, some of you, from mere force of habit, will doubtless contend that those saints appeared in the very same old fleshly bodies which they had once inhabited, and which, after their death, had crumbled to dust in the grave. Admitting that this your totally unwarranted assumption be correct, did those saints come forth from their graves naked, and go thus "into the holy city," or were they clothed? If clothed, where did they get their clothes, and how did they manage to pay for them? Were their old clothes resurrected as well as their old bodies? If so, why do you not preach the resurrection of old clothes as well of old bodies? If their old clothes were not resurrected at the same time with their old bodies, then, of necessity, those saints must have come forth from their graves naked, and must, in that utterly destitute condition, have entered "into the holy city, and appeared unto many." And what finally became of them? Did they procure clothes, resume their old occupations, and afterwards die for the second time, or did they, all naked as they then were, strike right out up to your imaginary heaven? That they remained among men, and suffered death a second time, you will hardly venture to assert. Of necessity, then, we have before us the strange spectacle of a whole troop of naked saints, with material bodies just like our own, mounting up in the air, trying to reach your heaven. But how high could saints, with such bodies, get, without ladders, and how could they, thus naked, endure the intense cold of the upper regions? Besides all this, those saints would meet with another very serious difficulty. The earth is known to move forward in her orbit at a rate of motion sixty times greater than that of a cannon ball. Unless, then, your heaven be connected with the earth, and accompany her in her journey around the sun, it is evident that the moment those saints, in starting to heaven, took their feet off the ground the earth would pass from under them, leaving them far behind in her wake, dangling in space, with nothing to guide them in their new and perilous journey. How supremely ridiculous your pagan teachings become in the light of modern science!

Without involving all these and many more similar absurdities, those saints could have been nothing else than spirits. That they actually were spirits is also fully made apparent by the phraseology of the language used in describing them. It is not said of them that they were seen by many, but that they "appeared unto many." The verb "appeared," being in the active voice, shows that it was, by an action or effort, on their own part, that those saints became visible to men. Had they possessed material bodies, like ours, visible at all times, no effort on their own part would have been necessary in order to render themselves visible. In that case it would not have been proper to say of them that they "appeared." They would have been passive objects of vision, and it would have been said of them that they were seen. In speaking of material objects, such as men, dogs, horses, etc., we always say that we have seen them, never that they have "appeared unto" us. In speaking of ethereal objects, however, such as spirits, we may, very properly, say that they have "appeared unto" us. In its active sense, as used in the text, the verb appear is used only in connection with objects which are usually invisible, and which, when they do appear, are called apparitions. In this active sense men, in material bodies, never appear, and hence they are never called apparitions. This is the very sense, however, in which spirits do appear, and hence they are always called apparitions. Previous to the time alluded to the saints in question had been invisible. Then, as apparitions, they suddenly "appeared unto many." Then again, as is usual with apparitions, they just as suddenly disappeared. Beyond all question, then, they were spirits in spiritual bodies; and the many unto whom they appeared were seeing mediums.

In this affair I have now made out a clear case of the reappearance of the dead, in the form of spirits.

This event occurred after the resurrection of Jesus. Since, then, in rising from the dead and reappearing unto men, Jesus became "the first fruits of them that slept," we have an assurance that all who have slept in death are empowered to thus rise up and reappear.

And now, let me ask, if, with your present views, you had lived at the time of which I am speaking, would you have believed the report of the "many" who professed to have witnessed the reappearance, in spirit form, of those departed saints? Or, if those same persons were living now, and were to make a similar report, would you believe their report? If not—if you would not believe it, though received directly from the witnesses themselves—how can you believe it at all? If the story, direct from the lips of the witnesses, was unworthy of credit, can it have become worthy by reaching us, as it does, through hearsay handed down to us through numberless copyings and translations? Do we know anything of the character for skill and honesty of the copyists, the translators, and the priests through whose hands the story has reached us? If, however, in regard to such a matter, you would receive the report of a set of Jews totally unknown to you, if you do receive that report, as it reaches us through a thousand doubtful channels, how can you so promptly reject the direct testimony to the same effect of still greater numbers of the most truthful and intelligent persons of the present time? Do you not perceive that in thus accepting the weaker and rejecting the stronger testimony you are acting very inconsistently? Be all this as it may, however, you accept the story as it reaches us, and in this story we have positive evidence, not only of the truth of Spiritualism, but also of the fact that it was employed by heaven on this occasion to give additional grandeur, solemnity, and significance to the resurrection of Jesus, and to the ushering in of the Christian Dispensation.

All this is equally true, no matter in what kind of bodies those saints reappeared. In order to reappear at all, they had, of course, to return to earth from the place of their abode in the world of spirits. In order to know when to return, to what place, and in what manner, the spirits of those saints had equally, of course, to be fully cognizant of all that was transpiring on earth. Since, then, the laws of our being never change, it is evident that by whatever laws those saints, while in spirit life, were then enabled to know what was transpiring on earth, and to reappear to men, by the same laws, they must still be enabled to know the same things and to reappear in the same manner. You are bound to admit, therefore, all the teachings of Spiritualism, or else deny that spirits ever did reappear on that or on any other occasion.

In Luke xxiv, 37, we read: "But they were terrified and affrighted, and supposed that they had seen a spirit." This is spoken of the disciples of Jesus on the occasion of his first reappearance to them after his resurrection. You will doubtless claim, however, that on this occasion the disciples were deceived; that what they mistook for a spirit was not a spirit at all, and that consequently this case does nothing to establish the truth of Spiritualism. Admitting, however, that on this particular occasion they were deceived, I still prove that the disciples were all firm believers in Spiritualism. They firmly believed that what they saw was a spirit making its appearance unto them. Could they have believed this if they had not believed that spirits could and did thus appear to men? And is the firm faith of these men worth nothing? Were they likely to adopt a belief on insufficient evidence? If they were, then probably all those beliefs in which you follow them were adopted on insufficient evidence. If, in regard to Spiritualism, they erred, have we any assurance that they did not equally err in regard to the whole subject of Christianity? Were they any more liable to err in the former case than in the latter? And are you going to condemn them for their belief in Spiritualism just as you condemn us for the same belief? If in them that belief was no crime, can it be a crime in us?

Be this as it may, however, are you prepared to prove that the belief of the disciples in the power of spirits to appear unto men was an erroneous belief? They made a mistake, you say, on this occasion in supposing that a certain person was a spirit, when he was not. But does this one mistake—if it was a mistake—prove that spirits are never seen at all? If I make a mistake in supposing that a certain object is a horse, when, in fact, it is some other kind of animal, does my one mistake prove that horses never can be seen at all? Your argument proves nothing, and if it did—if it fully established the fact that the apostles did entertain and teach erroneous doctrines—would not your proof be as fatal to Christianity as to Spiritualism?

If, in regard to the power of spirits to appear unto

men, the apostles had been in error, would not Jesus have corrected that error? Can it be possible that he, too, fell into an error in regard to this matter? Be this as it may, so far from even intimating that the apostles held erroneous views in regard to this matter, he proceeds to confirm their views by speaking of the appearance of spirits, the nature of their bodies, etc., as of things with which he supposes them to be fully acquainted. He further confirms their views by calling their attention to several points in which he differs, or, at least, seems to differ, from a spirit. Thus you see that, even admitting that Jesus was not at that time a spirit, I make a strong case in favor of the truth of Spiritualism.

But upon what authority do you base your assertion that, at the time referred to, Jesus was not a spirit? Did he say that he was not? On the contrary, when not perverted to sustain some man-made creed, his peculiar phraseology shows clearly that he was a spirit, and that he wished his disciples to have a correct knowledge of him as such. When he saw them affrighted at his sudden appearance in their midst, when he perceived the conflicting thoughts that arose in their minds concerning his identity, his present nature, etc., "he said unto them, Why are ye troubled? and why do thoughts arise in your hearts? Behold my hands and my feet that it is I myself: handle me, and see, for a spirit hath not flesh and bones, as ye see me have." As to whether he was a spirit or not there seems to have been no question in the minds of the disciples. From the moment of his appearance among them they were satisfied in regard to this matter. That he was a spirit they did not doubt. Without having been visible as he approached them, he suddenly "stood in the midst of them." They knew that no one but a spirit, a genuine apparition, could have appeared in that manner. Seeing that they were correct in recognizing him as a spirit, Jesus said nothing to them in regard to that matter. Had they erred, however, in that respect, he certainly would have corrected their error.

The only questions in their minds were in regard to his identity and to the nature of his spiritual body. The question in regard to his identity he settled by the showing of his hands and his feet; that in regard to the nature of his body by having his disciples handle him. It was of the utmost importance that these two questions should be correctly settled in the minds of the apostles; that concerning his identity in order that through their teachings the world might know that he did, in very deed, arise from the dead; that concerning the nature of his body in order that the world, in like manner, might know the nature of the body of the saints "in the resurrection," of whom he was "the first fruits," and the model. As he then was the saints were to be.

To the sight of the apostles the body of Jesus seemed to be composed of flesh and bones. Had he said nothing on the subject, therefore, they would doubtless have believed, as many of you do believe, that such was the fact, and would have taught the world that such was the composition of the bodies of all spirits. Perceiving their mistake, however, and wishing to correct it, Jesus requested them to handle him, "for," said he, " a spirit hath not flesh and bones as ye see me have." He did not say flesh and bones as he had, but, as to their sight, he seemed to have. He wished them to understand that his flesh and bones existed, not in reality, but only in appearance. Had the evidence of their sight been correct in regard to these things they would have needed no other evidence. In that case Jesus would have acted very absurdly in having them handle him. As well might I ask you to handle me to convince yourselves that I have flesh and bones, when the evidence of your sight has already correctly made known to you that fact. Were I a spirit, however, and were I to perceive that your sight deceived you in regard to the nature of my body, then, to correct that deception, I would have you do the very thing which Jesus, to correct just such an optical deception, had his disciples do—I would have you handle me. Having thus obtained a correct knowledge of the nature of the new body of Jesus, the apostles went forth and taught the world that, no matter how it may appear to the eye, the resurrected body is a spiritual body, and not the natural body of flesh and bones which is laid aside in death.

I am well aware that the view which I take of this subject is a novel one, and that it comes in direct conflict with the whole body of modern priestcraft. I am aware that most persons, blinded by this system of priestcraft, have been misled into the belief that Jesus had his disciples handle him to convince themselves that he had flesh and bones, as they saw that he had. But if he really had flesh and bones, and the disciples had correctly seen that he had them, what need was there for them to handle him in order to ascertain this already established and undisputed fact? Were you to show me a real apple, would you have me handle it in order to convince myself that it was a real apple, when my sight had already made known to me that fact? Were you, however, to show me a fine imitation of an apple, and were to see that I mistook it for a real apple, you would then have me handle it to convince myself that my eyes had deceived me, and that it had not the composition of a real apple, as, to my sight, it seemed to have. In this very way Jesus had to undeceive his disciples, when they mistook a fine imitation for a real human body.

To carry this illustration still further, you have two small boys look at each other through a pane of common window-glass. Each one correctly sees the other on the opposite side of the glass. In this case would you have either of the boys handle his companion in order to convince himself that his companion was really there? So of the body of Jesus. Had the flesh and the bones, which they saw it have, been real, there would have been no handling in the case. You may show these little boys a looking-glass. They see it have little boys on the other side of it. In this case, however, you tell them to handle what they see, and undeceive themselves, for the glass has not little boys on the other side, as they see it have. You surely would not have them do this handling to convince themselves that the looking-glass actually had little boys on the other side, as they saw it have. So of Jesus. He surely did not have his disciples handle the flesh and the bones which they saw him have, to convince themselves that those objects were really what they seemed.

You show these little boys a rod broken in the middle. They see that it is broken, and do not need to handle it to ascertain that fact. You now place a straight rod obliquely in a body of clear water. The little boys see this rod to be broken at the surface of the water. In this case, however, you tell them to handle the rod and undeceive themselves, for it is not broken, as they see it to be. You surely would not have them handle it to convince themselves that it actually was broken, as they saw it to be. So again of the body of Jesus. You call these little boys to look upon a beautiful rainbow. They see it have ends resting upon the ground, at no great distance. You tell them to go and handle the rainbow, for it has not ends resting on the ground, as they see it have. In this case, as in all the others, the handling is done to correct an optical illusion. So, once more, of the body of Jesus. The disciples were required to handle it to convince themselves that spirits, like himself, had not flesh and bones, as to the deceived sight he seemed to have.

Besides all these things it was on this very occasion, and just as he then was, that Jesus ascended into heaven, "and sat on the right hand of God." And are you prepared to maintain that he sits there now in a material body of literal flesh and bones? Paul positively declares that "flesh and blood cannot inherit the kingdom of heaven." Jesus also, on this same occasion, after having his disciples handle him, said : "These are the words which I spake unto you while I was yet with you." This language shows that he was no longer with them, and that he had now made them understand this fact. But in what sense was he no longer with them? Was he not, at that very moment, present in the room with them? Could his absence or separation from them have meant anything else than that he was no longer present with them in the natural body? Had he still possessed his old body of flesh and bones he would at that moment have been present with them in every sense in which he had ever been presant. In that case his speaking of being no longer with them would have been meaningless and silly.

"But," you ask, "if Jesus did not rise from the dead, and go to heaven in his old body of flesh and bones that had suffered on the cross, what became of that body?" This is a fair question, and one easily answered. That body, like all other dead bodies not artificially preserved, returned to dust. I base this answer upon the authority of science, which has never been known to lie. "But how came that body to be missing from the sepulcher in which it was placed when taken down from the cross?" This question I cannot answer. That body was not given into my charge. Those into whose charge it was given, however, testified that during the night the disciples came and stole it away; and this testimony was generally accepted by the Jews, who were best prepared to judge correctly concerning the matter. "But the guards," you say, "were bribed to make this report." Very likely they were, and it is equally likely that they had previously been bribed to let the disciples do the very thing set forth in this report. The disciples very well knew that it would never do to let that body remain over three days in the sepulcher. Within that time they must, by some means, obtain the body, and obtain it, too, in such a way as to create the impression upon the minds of the people that it had returned to life. What is more probable, then, than that they would try the effect of gold upon the unscrupulous, bribe-taking knaves who were on guard at the sepulcher? That something of the kind was done appears still more probable from the fact that the body, which, according to Jesus's own prediction, should have remained in the sepulcher three days, was made to rise after only one day. The disciples doubtless knew the right set of guards to deal with, and were afraid that this set might not all be on duty at the end of the three days. At any rate, it would be a very easy matter, at the present time, to obtain a body from so base a set of bribe-taking knaves as those guards evidently were. "But these guards testified that the theft was committed while they were asleep." Very well. Would it have done for them to testify that they had permitted this to be done while they were awake? Was not the plea that they had unintentionally fallen asleep the only plea for their neglect of duty which they could have made? Be all this as it may, however, it seems to me much more likely that the body was removed by human means than that it returned to life, and ascended into heaven. Many other bodies, some dead and some alive, have been mysteriously spirited away, under far greater difficulties than existed in the case of Jesus, and yet no one claims that any of these bodies ever ascended into heaven.

All those persons whose natural bodies have ever

been resuscitated or raised from the dead have become, after their resuscitation, just as they were before their temporary decease, and all of them have passed a second time through the change called death. None of them have ever gone from earth in their material bodies. Indeed, Paul declares that even those saints who may be on earth when the last trump shall sound shall not enter heaven in their fleshly bodies; but, in the twinkling of an eye, shall be changed, their natural and corruptible bodies for spiritual and incorruptible bodies, in which alone they can enter heaven. If, then, the natural and corruptible body of Jesus, after having perished upon the cross, was ever resuscitated, and was never again subjected to the change called death, then, of necessity, that body must have passed, in the twinkling of an eye, through the wonderful change of which Paul speaks, and thus become a spiritual and incorruptible body. "Flesh and blood cannot enter the kingdom of heaven."

From all these things we learn that, at the time of which we are speaking, Jesus was clothed, not in a corruptible body of flesh and bones, as to the deceived sight he seemed to be, but in a spiritual and incorruptible body, like unto the bodies of "the angels which are in heaven," and of "the spirits of just men made perfect." In other words, I have now proved beyond all possibility of contradiction that, after his resurrection, Jesus was a pure spirit. Like other spirits, he became visible and invisible at pleasure; he entered into, and passed out of, rooms with closed doors; and, finally, in direct opposition to the law of gravitation, he ascended from earth into heaven. If at that time he was not a spirit, what was he? You are forced to admit that he was then, as he is now, a spirit; and since, as the apostles afterward declared, God has never been seen, you are forced to admit also that the part of Jesus which was visible to men was his human part. In other words, you are forced to admit that, as seen by men after his resurrection, Jesus was a human spirit.

In my last lecture I proved that, while yet in the body, Jesus called up spirits, and conversed with them. By thus practicing Spiritualism himself, in the presence of those who were to be the founders of his church, he not only demonstrated its truth, but, also, by thus fixing upon it his seal of approval, forever settled the question as to its propriety. He was then acting from our own side of the great river of death, and being our ensample in this, as in all other things, he thus taught us to commune, at pleasure, with the beautiful beings on the other shore. Then, when he had passed over this great and mysterious river, and had himself thus become a spirit, he again taught Spiritualism from the other side by frequent communications with the loved ones he had left behind. Thus by his own example, acting in turn from both sides of the river of death, he taught Spiritualism to the inhabitants of our own world, and of the world of spirits. "The saints which slept," acting upon his example, began at once to make their appearance among men.

"To them that believe on his name" Jesus gave power to do all the works which he did, and even "greater works than these." This gift includes the power to communicate with spirits while we remain men, and to communicate with men when we become spirits. These were among the works that Jesus did, and, in the doing of these and other similar works, he promised to be with "them that believe," "alway, even unto the end of the world."

How dare you, then, pretend to be a believer in the teachings of Jesus, and yet denounce all these his promised works as humbugs, and of the devil? Had you lived in the time of Jesus, how supremely ridiculous you would have made himself and his teachings appear! And, were he now to appear among us, humble as he then was, and were to go about as he then did, teaching Spiritualism, how promptly, and with what ineffable scorn, you would brand him as a miserable "humbug." His followers were then, as they are now, almost entirely composed of irreligious persons. Many of them were outcasts from society. The professors of religion almost unanimously rejected him as a deceiver, a glutton, a wine-bibber, etc. This they did, partly because he went about in soiled garments, ate with unwashed hands, and associated with a class of people who were not admitted into good society. They did it principally, however, because, with arguments which they could not answer, he boldly attacked their favorite dogmas. These were not really wicked men. They were members of the orthodox church, the custodians and expounders of the scriptures, the owners of the wealth of the nation, the guardians of morality, the devout worshipers of the only true God. In short, they were just what the best class of orthodox religionists are to-day — well-meaning bigots. They opposed Jesus, not from wicked motives, but because they believed that his teachings and his example were calculated to overturn the institutions of society, promote vagrancy and immorality, and diminish the respect due to religion. They did just as you would have done had you been in their places; just as you would now do were Jesus to come among us, and act just as he did then. In short, these high-toned and devout champions of the Bible, of morality, and of orthodoxy, treated Jesus just as you, to the fullest extent of your power, do now treat me, and all others who, like Jesus, dare boldly attack error whenever found, and who, with arguments which you cannot answer, are establishing grand and beautiful truths, and who are threatening the overthrow of many of your man-made, your priest-paying, your soul-dwarfing, your time-rotten religious dogmas.

In Rev. iii, 20, we read: "Behold, I stand at the door and knock: if any man hear my voice, and open the door, I will come in to him, and will sup with him, and he with me." This was spoken by Jesus long after he had become a spirit. If, then, he speaks the truth, and actually does stand and knock or rap upon our doors, are not his rappings genuine spirit rappings?

Because from your childhood up you have been so taught, by unscrupulous priests who bend all scriptures to suit their own creeds, you will, as a matter of course, contend that on this occasion Jesus did not mean what he said, nor say what he meant; that when he said the door he meant the heart, etc. In reply to all this I will say that Jesus probably understood the meaning he intended to express fully as well as you understand it, and that he probably used the proper words to express that meaning. Had he on this occasion meant the heart, he would doubtless, as on other occasions, have used the word heart to express that meaning. Besides this, a heart is not so convenient a thing to "stand at," and to "knock" upon, as is a door, nor do men enter in through hearts to "sup." If you change the word door, in the text, to heart, you are bound also to make a corresponding change in all the other words of the sentence. Then, of course, you will have a text supporting your own creed, but made entirely by yourself and with your own meaning; not a text made by Jesus, with his meaning.

The changing of texts in this manner, or, rather, the doing away with them entirely, and the making of new texts in their places, has been found extremely convenient in the propping up of their respective creeds by all the different denominations of Christians. They have all made a liberal use of this privilege, and by so doing have filled the world with interminable wranglings, and have on many occasions filled all the nations of Christendom with the most horrible scenes of carnage.

They can all easily agree to do away with Bible texts, and Bible meanings; but over the creed-texts, and creed-meanings, which are substituted for these, they always quarrel; and frequently, for the love of the merciful Jesus, they mercilessly cut one anothers' throats by the tens of thousands at once. Every historian knows that these are simple historical facts. And yet you persist in a course which you very well know has been the cause of countless and unspeakable evils. Is it not just as unfair to charge Jesus with meaning heart, when he says door, as it would be to charge him with meaning door, when he says heart? Taking the text, however, as made by yourself, are not the knockings or influences of the spirit Jesus upon the heart just as genuine and just as wonderful spiritual manifestations as would be any literal rappings upon a real door? With any meaning, therefore, that can possibly be given to its language, I have, in this text, established a genuine case of spiritual communication—a case, too, which you dare not, according to your custom, stigmatize as of the devil.

In Rev. vii, 9, we read: "After this I beheld, and lo, a great multitude, which no man could number, of all nations, and kindreds, and people, and tongues, stood before the throne, and before the Lamb, clothed in white robes, and palms in their hands." If John tells the truth, as he probably does, he actually did see all those innumerable hosts of spirits. As he tells us in another place, he also actually heard their voices. If he really did see all these spirits, and hear their voices, was he not a wonderful spiritual medium? Was this case of the devil? What would you think of John, if he were living now, a near neighbor to you, and were to report that he had seen and heard so many spirits? Would you not put him down as an impostor or an insane person? And was he any less an impostor, any less an insane man, when he did report these things than he would be were he to report them now? Letting all these things pass, however, how far from the earth could those spirits have been, and yet have been so distinctly seen and heard by him? And, by the same power that then enabled John to see and to hear spirits, may not men now be enabled, in like manner, to see and to hear them? Have either men or spirits, since John's time, been deprived of any of their powers or capacities?

Forced to admit that Spiritualism did prevail among the Jews and the founders of the Christian Church, you now resort, in your desperation, to the totally unfounded assumption that all spiritual manifestations ceased soon after the time of the apostles. You would doubtless be glad to deny that Spiritualism ever did prevail at all among the Jews, the apostles, or any others. To deny this, however, would be, as you well know, to deny the truth of the whole Bible, and to leave no foundation at all for your own religion. The best you can do, therefore, is to assume that, although spiritual manifestations did once prevail, God discovered that they did not pay, and that consequently he caused them all to cease. In resorting to this assumption, however, you make liars of Jesus and the apostles, who declared that these signs should "follow them that believe," "alway, even unto the end of the world." You also make liars of all the fathers of the church, of all the saints, of all the martyrs, and of all the historians down, at least, to the time of the so-called Reformation. You also make liars of Luther, of Melancthon, of Zwinglius, of Calvin, of Wesley, of Clarke—of nearly all, in fact, of the great lights and the great leaders of your own churches. You make liars, too, of countless thousands of the most truthful and intelligent persons, of all nations, and of all religions, of the present age. All of these grand witnesses testify that spiritual manifestations have never been absent from among men. And should your totally unsupported assumption that all these manifestations have ceased weigh more with us than this mighty accumulation of the testimony of all nations, of all religions, and of all ages?

Because you happen never to have seen or to have communed with a spirit yourself, you contend that the seeing of spirits, and the communing with them, ceased about eighteen hundred years ago. So, because I happen never to have seen a lion, or to have heard one roar, I contend, with equal reason, that the seeing of lions, and the hearing of them roar, ceased about eighteen hundred years ago. Our cases are exactly parallel, our conclusions equally reasonable. Negative testimony proves nothing at all. The positive testimony of one good witness to the effect that he has seen a lion, or a spirit, is worth more than the negative testimony of a million equally good witnesses to the effect that they have not seen any such thing.

Time will not permit me to give even a thousandth part of the testimony in favor of Spiritualism which is to be found within the domain of the Christian Church. I will add enough, however, to that already given, to fully satisfy all those whom priestcraft has not rendered incapable of reasoning on such matters that Spiritualism is, indeed, a glorious reality.

Justin Martyr, who died in 161, says that the incarnation took place "for the sake of unbelievers, and for the overthrow of evil spirits." He then adds: "You may know this now from what passes before your eyes; for many demoniacs all over the world, and in your own metropolis, whom none other exorcists, conjurers, or sorcerers have cured, these have many of our Christians cured, adjuring by the name of Christ, and still do cure." Again he says: "With us, even hitherto, are prophetic gifts, from which you Jews ought to gather, that what formerly belonged to your race is transferred to us." Elsewhere he says: "With us may be seen both males and females, with gifts from the spirit of God."

Irenæus, who suffered martyrdom in 202, says: "Some most certainly and truly cast out demons, so that frequently those persons themselves that were cleansed from wicked spirits believed and were received into the church. Others have the knowledge of things to come, as also visions and prophetic communications. Others heal the sick by the interposition of hands, and restore them to health." In another place he says: "We hear of many of the brethren in the church who have prophetic gifts, and who speak in all tongues through the spirit, and who also bring to light the secret things of men for their benefit, and who expound the mysteries of God." These extracts are given as quoted by Eusebius, and show that spiritual phenomena were still prevalent in the Church at the close of the second century.

Tertullian, the most eloquent father of the second century, in his work "De Amma," says: "We had a right, after what was said by St. John, to expect prophesyings; and we not only acknowledge these spiritual gifts, but we are permitted to enjoy the gifts of a prophetess. There is a sister among us who possesses the faculty of revelation. She commonly, during our religious service, on the Sabbath, falls into a crisis or trance. She has then intercourse with the angels, sees sometimes the Lord himself, sees and hears divine mysteries, and discovers the hearts of some persons; and administers medicine to such as desire it." After adding much more, all to the same effect, he says that on one occasion, after the close of the service, "she informed us that she had seen a soul in bodily shape; that it appeared to be a spirit, but not empty or formless, or wanting a living constitution, but that its form appeared so substantial that you might touch or hold it. It was tender, shining, of the color of air, but in everything resembling the human form." Here, then, near the close of the second century, we have a genuine Spiritualist—a well-developed, seeing, hearing, and healing medium, holding her seances in the church during the religious services; and yet we see her receiving the highest marks of confidence and respect from this great father, and from all the members of the church, who looked upon her mediumistic powers, thus exercised among them, as special favors from heaven. How promptly you would put a stop to such proceedings should they be attempted in those gorgeous resorts of pride and of fashion which you absurdly call your churches! In another place Tertullian says: "Exorcists appeal to the power of angels and demons, who prophesy through goats and tables." We all know what is meant by prophesying through tables. In regard to the goats, however, the meaning is not so clear.

St. Cyprian, who suffered martyrdom in 258, confirms all this testimony, and adds much more of a similar character. He relates that on one occasion, while quite awake, he had a vision of a young man of more than mortal stature, who showed him himself, led before the proconsul, and condemned to die as a martyr to Christianity. He recorded his vision, and it was afterward fulfilled to the letter.

St. Augustine, St. Jerome, and many others testify to the continuance of spiritual manifestations in the church during the fourth and the fifth centuries. Among many other things of a similar nature, St. Augustine, in his work, "De Cura pro Mortuis," declares that the spirit of the martyr Felix appeared at Nota. St. Jerome taught that the spirits of the saints are everywhere doing the work of the Savior. In his reply to an opposer of Spiritualism, he asks: "What dost thou mean? Wilt thou prescribe laws to God? Are the apostles to remain bound in chains till the day of judgment? Is it not written of them that they shall follow the Lamb everywhere? Is the Lamb then everywhere? Then they are everywhere, too, and where they will." What do you think of this brave and eloquent old Spiritualist?

Sozomen relates that an evil spirit, in the form of a beautiful woman, appeared to a noted theurgist, by the name of Apelles, who struck it in the face with a hot iron. This was certainly a very remarkable spiritual manifestation. Apelles, however, was guilty of a very ungallant act in striking the spirit in its face. I would not treat anything that way that would come to me in the form of a beautiful woman.

In his fortieth sermon St. Ambrose declares that the martyr Agnes was seen one night at her grave, surrounded by a choir of singing maidens. Was not that a spiritual manifestation? Eusebius relates that a certain officer, Basilides, was converted to Christianity by the spirit of the martyr Potamiæna. Basilides had shown her kindness at the time of her execution, and she promised that after her death she would appear to him. She did thus appear in consequence, and he became a Christian. Was not this a case of Spiritualism? And was it of the devil?

St. Gregory gives many instances of the appearing of spirits, both good and bad. Origen contends that the spirits of bad men are bound to the earth by their base and earthly desires, and that they often appear to men and disturb them. Irenæus bears witness to the same things, as do also St. Augustine, Chrysostom, Theodoret, and hosts of others, the great lights, the heroes of Christianity. Indeed, as the great moral philosopher, John Locke, says, you must destroy the authority, and the common honesty, of all the fathers, or admit the continuance of spiritual manifestations.

And dare you undertake to prove that all the fathers, all the saints, all the martyrs, and all the historians of the first six centuries were liars, totally devoid of common honesty? If not, then you are bound to admit that Spiritualism, in all its phases, did prevail in the Christian Church during all those centuries. And did all spiritual phenomena cease after the close of the sixth century? The unanimous voice of the whole church and of the whole world for the next thousand years, emphatically answers, "No!!" For want of time I cannot, at present, notice any portion of this vast accumulation of testimony.

It now devolves upon you to show when all spiritual phenomena ceased, why they all ceased, by whose authority they all ceased, by what means they were made to cease, and why they may not have been recommenced in our own time. Can you show any of these things? If not, what becomes of your baseless assumption that all of these phenomena have ceased? Where are the spirits now, and how are they confined to keep them from communing with men, as they did in earlier times? You say that the good spirits are in heaven, the wicked spirits in hell. But what and where are heaven and hell, and what modern improvements have been made in them to keep their inhabitants from communing, as they formerly did, with the inhabitants of earth? And is Jesus also confined in heaven? Is he never present, on earth, at your revivals, your camp-meetings, etc.? If he is present at these places, is he never accompanied by spirits? If not, then we have succeeded in proving John a monstrous liar, for in Rev. xiv, 4, he describes a host of spirits, and says: "These are they which follow the Lamb withersoever he goeth. They were redeemed from among men," etc. If Jesus is not present at your revivals, etc., are not your churches, from beginning to end, enormous swindling concerns? If you admit that Jesus is sometimes present at your meetings, you are bound to admit also that on those occasions, as well as on all others, he is accompanied by those spirits " which follow " him " whithersoever he goeth." In making these admissions, however, you admit not only the truth, but also the glorious nature of Spiritualism. If you deny all these things, then you are bound to admit that yourselves are a set of shameless impostors, and unmitigated scoundrels. Which one of these unpleasant admissions will you make?

Calmet, who wrote less than two hundred years ago, says: "We have in history several instances of persons, full of religion and piety, who, in the fervor of their orisons, have been taken up into the air, and remained there for some time. We have known a good monk who rises sometimes from the ground, and remains suspended without wishing it, without seeking to do so, especially on seeing some devotional image, or on hearing some devout prayer, such as 'Gloria in Excelsis Deo.' I know a nun to whom it has happened, in spite of herself, to see herself thus raised up in the air to a certain distance from the earth." He also says that this same thing occurred to St. Philip of Neri, to St. Catharine Columbina, and to Loyola, who "was raised up from the ground to the height of two feet, while his body shone like light." St. Dunstan, Archbishop of Canterbury, was thus elevated in the presence of many witnesses. In 1036 Richard, Abbot of St. Vanne de Verdun, was thus elevated in the presence of the Duke Galizan and his sons, and a great number of lords and ladies. Among many others who were thus elevated were St. Robert de Palentin, St. Philip Benitas, St. Cajatanus, St. Albert of Sicily, St. Francis of Assissium, St. Dominic, founder of the order of preaching brothers, and Savonarola, who was afterward put to death for becoming a Protestant. St. Theresa relates of herself that she was thus raised up from the ground. And now, let me ask, if all these persons, or if any of them, were thus raised up by spirit power, why may not persons of our own time be raised up in the same manner by the same power?

Catholics will not deny any of the spiritual manifestations which I have mentioned, nor any of the thousands of other well authenticated cases which I could give from Catholic writers, famous alike for their learning, their intelligence, and the purity of their lives. As an evidence that they are the true church of Christ, Catholics always have claimed to possess all those spiritual gifts promised by Jesus to "them that believe." It is this Spritualism, too, among Catholics which, notwithstanding their many imperfections, gives them life, and union, and strength. On the other hand, it is the want of this Spiritualism among Protestants which, notwithstanding their many perfections, causes them to be all broken up into a thousand hostile sects or factions, which, by their constant wranglings, and their countless contradictions, are doing more to make infidels than are all other influences combined.

You claim, however, that all the cases of spiritual manifestation which I have given, from the writers of the church, are lies invented by Catholics. This may be true; but in that case, what becomes of your New Testament? It was gotten up and put before the world by these same lying Catholics. This was done, too, at a time when, according to your own account, they were specially active in manufacturing the lies in question. As most of you doubtless know, the New Testament was compiled from a vast multitude of conflicting gospels, epistles, etc., by the first council of Nice, in the early part of the fourth century. Athanasius was the leader of the orthodox division of that council, and was the framer of your orthodox or Athanasian creed; and yet, few men, if any, ever manufactured and left on record a greater number of the so-called lies in question than did he. Indeed, we find a greater or less number of those so-called lies in the works of every member of that council whose writings have reached our own time. The orthodox division of that council, whom you follow, all agreed in palming off the lies in question upon the world, and in honoring, as most noted for piety, the men who manufactured the greatest number of these lies. And do you suppose that a council, composed of men so far gone in the vice of lying, would fail to supply the New Testament with a goodly number of these lies? Would they not be sure to so get this book up that it would correspond with their other books which were all filled with lies? What assurance, then, have you that your New Testament is not filled with Catholic lies? Better investigate this matter.

According to your own arguments, the spiritual manifestations recorded by Calmet and other recent writers, whose works have not been tampered with, are really better authenticated than are any of those recorded in the New Testament, and the objections which you urge against the writings of these, and of other eminent Catholic authors, bear with increased weight against the writings of the New Testament. Destroy the authenticity of the one set of these writings, then, yourselves, and infidels, adopting your own arguments, will quickly destroy the authenticity of the other set.

But do Catholics never tell the truth? Have they

not always been, and are they not now, devoted Christians? And does Christianity tend to make unmitigated liars of all its devotees? How does it happen that you Protestants are all so wonderfully truthful, when you are devoted to the same religion, and when you so recently formed a part of a people so wofully addicted to lying? Is not human nature the same in you that it is in them? What have you that you did not receive from them? Are you not a branch from the great Catholic tree? And can a branch differ in its nature from the tree which produces it? Take away all that you have received from Catholics, and what will you have left? Absolutely nothing, except a few negative doctrines—denials of miracles, etc., for which you are indebted to the great infidel writers of France and of Germany. And is it to infidelity that you owe your superior truthfulness? If not, to what do you owe it? For my life I cannot see any good reason why you should be so much better every way than are your Catholic Christian brethren. Whatever the reason may be, however, the fact stares us in the face that you never lie, and that your great leaders are necessarily first-class witnesses in any case in which they are called upon to testify. Let us see, then, what they have to say on the subject of Spiritualism.

Dr. Conyers Middleton, your great anti-miracle champion, says: "It must be confessed that the claim to a miraculous power was universally asserted and believed in all Christian countries, and in all ages of the church, till the time of the Reformation, for ecclesiastical history makes no difference between one age and another, but carries on the succession of its miracles, as of other common events, through all of them indifferently to that memorable period. As far as church historians can illustrate anything, there is not a single point in all history so constantly, explicitly, and unanimously affirmed by them as the continual succession of those powers, through all ages, from the earliest father who first mentions them, down to the Reformation; which same succession is still further deduced by persons of the same eminent character for probity, learning, and dignity in the Romish church to this very day."

This is the language of one of the brightest lights of Protestantism—of a man of vast powers of mind and of immense learning; of a man, too, so intensely bitter in his opposition to the Catholic church, and to the doctrine of spiritual manifestations, that, while he admits the "eminent character for probity, learning, and dignity" of the fathers of the church and of other Catholic writers, he resolves to bring, and does bring, the charge of wholesale and unmitigated lying against them all, from the first father down to the latest writer of his own time. This he does, not because he believes the charge to be true, but because he believes that, in the war which Protestantism is carrying on against the Catholic church, such a charge is necessary. He fears, and with good reason, too, that by admitting that Catholics do still possess those spiritual gifts which, as signs, were to "follow them that believe," we should be forced to admit also, as we certainly would, that they constitute the true church of Christ. He says: "For if any credit be due them in the present case, it must reach to all or none; because the reason for believing them in any one age will be found to be of equal force in all, as far as it depends on the character of the persons attesting, or the thing attested. . . . By granting to the Romanists but a single age of miracles, after the time of the apostles, we shall be entangled in a series of difficulties whence we can never fairly extricate ourselves till we allow the same powers also to the present age." He blames those Protestant writers severely who admit that genuine miracles did continue to prevail during the first four or five centuries. He blames these writers, not because the admitted miracles were not genuine, but because, by admitting them to have been genuine, they have made a concession to the Catholic church, which, if allowed, would be fatal to Protestantism.

We now understand why it is that you, and nearly all other Protestants, so persistently deny the genuineness of all spiritual manifestations. You have no objection to the signs themselves, but you justly fear the thing signified by them. Admit that Spiritualists or any other people do possess genuine spiritual gifts, and you admit that they are of "them that believe," and of "them who shall be heirs of salvation." You know this, and being destitute of these signs yourselves, you feel that you appear in the rather unenviable light of mere pretenders. Hence your very natural desire to make others seem to be in the same condition. You are like the fox in the fable, who, having lost his own tail, in order to make the misfortune general, tried to deprive all the other foxes of their tails.

Unfortunately for you, however, your founder, the

great Luther himself, in the most positive manner, testifies to the truth of Spiritualism. His testimony is, of necessity, either true or false. If true, then by that testimony I prove that Spiritualism is true, and that it was present at the ushering in of Protestantism, just as it had been present at the ushering in of Christianity itself. If, however, his testimony be false, then Luther stands before us a convicted liar and impostor, and you stand before us the convicted followers of a liar and impostor. Which horn of this dilemma will you choose? If Luther lies in favor of Spiritualism, which he does not wish to establish, is he not sure to lie in favor of those things which he does wish to establish? If, then, we shall reject his testimony in favor of Spiritualism, is there not a double reason why we should reject his testimony in favor of Protestantism?

You have only to read his biography, or his own writings, to learn that he was accustomed, almost daily, to see spirits, and to hold conversations with them. It is true he regarded most of these as evil spirits, and treated them accordingly. He was so sorely afflicted with the devil-on-the-brain that whatever he could not clearly understand he at once, very naturally, attributed to the devil. This, however, does not in the least invalidate his testimony in regard to the genuineness of the manifestations themselves. Neither the character of the spirits themselves, nor that of the communications made by them, has anything to do in the case. The only question is, did Luther see spirits and converse with them at all? If he did, then no matter what may have been the character of those spirits, my case is gained, and Spiritualism is established. When I prove that spirits are in the habit of communicating with men, do I not prove that such communication is practicable? And if evil spirits have power to communicate in this manner, have not good spirits power to do the same? Dare you assert the absurd and blasphemous doctrine that God grants powers the most desirable, and privileges the most dear, to wicked spirits, who abuse them for the eternal ruin of men, while at the same time he denies these powers and these privileges to good spirits, who would use them for the eternal salvation of men? Does God thus reward the wicked, and punish the good? Could the devil do worse than this?

Luther, however, does not claim that all the spirits are evil, or that any of them are necessarily so, that communicate with men. On the contrary, he says: "I will not derogate from the gifts of others, if haply to any one, over and above scripture, God should reveal aught by dreams, by visions, or by angels." Sometimes the spirits that came to him were in angelic forms, and some of them gave him good advice, which he followed. A short time before the death of their daughter Magdalen, Mrs. Luther, in a vision, saw two beautiful youths, who came to ask her daughter in marriage. On relating her vision to Melancthon, he declared that the youths were angels come to convey the pure spirit of the girl to the true marriage of the heavenly kingdom. On that same day Magdalen died. Suspicious as he was in regard to the character of spirits, Luther never doubted that these two were good spirits. Indeed, when disputing with the Anabaptists, he required them to prove their authority by performing miracles. From this we learn that he regarded all those as impostors to whom were wanting those spiritual gifts promised to "them that believe." Speaking of the Swinkfeldians, he says: "If I must glory in what belongs to me, I have seen more spirits than they will see in a whole year."

Melancthon was also a Spiritualist, and a good medium. Indeed, without being both of these, no one can be successful as a religious leader. He often conversed with spirits. I will give only one instance. On this occasion the spirit appeared in the clear light of day, when several persons were present. A certain preacher, Grynæus, having by his criticisms offended another preacher, returned to his lodgings, and related the affair to Melancthon and others who sat at table with him. Soon Melancthon was called out to speak with a strange old man, well-dressed and of honest countenance, and who urged Melancthon to hurry Grynæus out of the city, and thus have him escape arrest at the hands of an officer who, instigated by the offended preacher, would come within an hour to conduct Grynæus to prison. Having delivered his message, the old man, or the spirit, as it proved to be, vanished out of sight.

In the Homilies of the Church of England we read: "The Holy Ghost doth always declare himself, by the word of wisdom, by the word of knowledge, which is the understanding of the scriptures; by faith in doing of miracles, by healing them that are diseased, by prophecy, by discerning of spirits. by the diversities of tongues," etc. Can all this be true, and yet Spiritualism be false?

The spiritual manifestations in the Wesley family, and the defense by the Wesleys of the doctrine of spiritual communications, are too well-known, and too well-authenticated, to require any notice from me. And were the Wesleys truthful men? If they were, then by their own testimony I prove the truth of Spiritualism. If they were not, then I prove many of you to be the followers of liars and impostors. Had I time, I could also prove the truth of Spiritualism by the testimony of John Calvin, John Knox, Alexander Campbell, and, in fact, by that of nearly all the others of your greatest and best leaders.

Dr. Adam Clarke says: "That the spirits of the dead might and did appear was a doctrine held by the greatest and holiest men that ever existed; and a doctrine which the cavillers, free-thinkers and bound-thinkers of different ages have never been able to disprove." With "the greatest and holiest men that ever existed" on our side, and with the full assurance that we have truth, also, on our side, need we fear your puny opposition?

You have a great deal to say about heaven; about the splendid mansions, the fine clothes, the musical instruments, etc., which you profess to own there. You talk loudly about going there yourselves, and try to get others hooked on to go along with you. And yet, as I have already shown, you have not the faintest idea as to where heaven is, or as to what it is, unless, as Spiritualists teach, it be here round about us, and consists alone in condition. Do you think that one of your most intelligent and most highly educated preachers could look you steadily in the face, and, without laughing, declare on the honor of a gentleman that he does truly believe all that which for money he preaches to you about this vague, this totally unlocatable heaven?

Since, according to your own teachings, all communication has been cut off between the spirit world and our own, how do new-born spirits from earth manage to get to your heaven? Can they pass over a way impassable to older and more experienced spirits? You say that they are borne thither by angels. But have I not already proved that many of the angels, if not all of them, are human beings, and that, at any rate, human spirits, acting as angels, have the same powers as have other angels? If, then, angels can come to earth, cannot human spirits do the same? And who would be more likely to come than would the relatives and the friends of the new-born spirit? Would not such spirits, too, while here, be very likely to make communications to men? And, whether the angels be human spirits or not, how do they know exactly when and where on earth their services are required? Does not such knowledge, on their part, prove the existence of a constant correspondence between the two worlds, or the two conditions? When men first die, where are their spirits? Here, of course, and here they are bound to remain till the next angel express train starts in the direction in which they propose to go. Spirits, then, can and do exist here for a time; and if for a time, why not always? Suppose that the roads should in some way get out of repair, and the angel express train be stopped. What then? Would all the new-born spirits perish—suffer annihilation—or would they not remain round about us, as did the spirits in former ages, before you had heaven moved away? In any conceivable case, except that of annihilation, are we not bound at times to have spirits about us?

Finally, how does your heaven—wherever it may be—retain its position in space? If by the law of gravitation, then it must be composed of matter, like the earth and other planetary bodies, and must also, like them, possess planetary motion. This would make it a planet, governed like the earth, by physical laws. Such, indeed, it is bound to be, if it possesses matter at all. If, however, it be entirely destitute of matter, then, of necessity, it must be a perfect vacuum, equivalent to nothing at all. Where, then, and what is your heaven, and in what are its inhabitants occupied, since you had them stopped from ministering to men? You cannot tell where your heaven is, nor what it is, but you can tell how its inhabitants are employed! "They are resting," you say, "loafing around the throne, singing hallelujahs, playing on golden harps, tooting on penny trumpets loaned them for that purpose," etc. Very well. But what have they done to make them either need or desire so much rest? And when, where, and how did the great majority of them acquire their wonderful taste for music, and so entirely lose their taste for everything else? To you such a place might be heaven, indeed; but to me so much noise and so much monotony would soon become intolerable. I would as lief try hell at once.

Without going outside of the Bible, and of the orthodox Christian church, I have now fully proved the truth of all the claims of Spiritualism. I have proved it by Luther, by Melancthon, by the Wesleys, by Middleton, and by Clarke. I have proved it by the unanimous testimony of all the fathers, of all the saints, of all the martyrs, of all the historians of the church, of all the evangelists, of all the apostles, and of Jesus himself. And now, in refutation of all this mighty accumulation of testimony, what have you to offer? You may cry, "Humbug! infidelity! blasphemy! down with him! great is Diana of the Ephesians! Hurrah for our church and our creeds!" You may persecute me, as others have done, and render my lot a hard one, and yet, will you thereby have answered any of my arguments, or rendered Spiritualism any the less true, any the less glorious?

LECTURE III.

SPIRITUALISM A NECESSITY IN GOD'S GENERAL GOVERNMENT.

Not believing in the existence of any such being as "God," I cannot, of course, believe in the existence of any such thing as "God's General Government." Having determined, however, to concede to my opponents everything claimed by them, I shall proceed in this lecture, as I proceeded in the two preceding lectures, on the hypothesis that there is a God, that he has a General Government, and that the teachings of the Bible and of the Christian church are all true. Then, using these teachings in favor of Spiritualism, I propose to compel my opponents, as I compelled them in the preceding two lectures, to either accept Spiritualism as fully established, or to impeach the testimony of their own witnesses.

In my two preceding lectures I fully established the truth of all the doctrines of Spiritualism. This I did exclusively on the testimony of the Bible and of the Christian church. In my present lecture I shall prove by the same witnesses that Spiritualism, in its various phases is an absolute necessity in the carrying on of God's General Government. In proving this I shall prove that Spiritualism is not only true, but is also of God, and not of the devil, as some of you have dared to blasphemously assert.

In Luke xv, 10, we read: "Likewise, I say unto you, there is joy in the presence of the angels of God over one sinner that repenteth." And now who are those persons that thus rejoice "in the presence of the angels of God?" The language evidently does not apply to the angels themselves, since the rejoicing is not represented as being done by them, but as being done by somebody else in their presence. The happy beings in question, then, can be no other than "the spirits of just men made perfect." These, and these only, dwell "in the presence of the angels of God." Indeed, it is highly probably, if not absolutely certain, that on any one occasion the rejoicing is principally done by the friends and the relatives of the particular "sinner that repenteth." This is the view that Christian Spiritualists take of this subject, and is the only view that involves no absurdities.

On account of their love for him, the friends and the relatives of the penitent would naturally feel a deep interest in his welfare, and would be watching over him, laboring and praying for his salvation. These persons would be much more likely than any others in the spirit world to know just when the sinner became penitent, and then, seeing that their prayers had been heard, that their labors had been rewarded, and that their loved one, whom they had feared would be lost, was coming to join them in their mansions of bliss, they would be sure to feel and to express a great amount of joy. If, then, the rejoicing be not done by these, by whom is it done?

Of necessity, it must be done on each occasion, either by all the inhabitants of heaven, or else by certain individuals only who have special reasons for rejoicing. But could it be done by all? Could untold billions of spirits, variously occupied, and in various places, all at the very same moment take cognizance of each individual case of penitence upon earth? In order to do this it would evidently be necessary for every inhabitant of heaven to have, at all times, a perfect knowledge of every action of every individual on earth, and of every circumstance surrounding him. Such knowledge, however, would be infinite, and hence could not be and is not possessed by finite beings, such as angels and "the spirits of just men made perfect." Since, then, the inhabitants of heaven cannot possibly all have knowledge of any one case of repentance, it follows, of necessity, that they cannot, and that they do not, all rejoice over any "one sinner that repenteth."

Suppose, however, that the countless hosts of heaven could, all at the same moment, have knowledge of every case of repentance on earth, would they, think you, on each of these occasions, all break forth together into ecstasies of joy? If so, would they have leisure for any other occupation, or room for any other joy? Would they ever get to rest from these rejoicings? Is there not some case of repentance on hand all the time? And would not this one source of joy, continuing thus ceaselessly and forever, finally become so common and so monotonous as to excite no special interest at all?

Suppose that the entire population of the earth could all, at the same moment, know that a certain sinner, a Hottentot, a Digger Indian, or an Esquimau, for instance, had repented, would any considerable number of them break forth into ecstasies of joy? When they hear of it, do the most zealous Christians among us ever give a second thought to any such case of repentance? And is it reasonable to suppose that the inhabitants of heaven feel much greater interest in such cases than do the inhabitants of earth?

From all this it is evident that the joy over any "one sinner that repenteth" must be confined principally to the comparatively few who have, in that particular case, some special reasons for rejoicing. This, indeed, is certainly the view which Jesus means to teach. Commencing at the fourth verse of the chapter in which the language in question is found, and including the tenth, which I have already quoted, we read: "What man of you having an hundred sheep, if he lose one of them, doth not leave the ninety and nine in the wilderness, and go after that which is lost, until he find it? And when he hath found it, he layeth it on his shoulders, rejoicing. And when he cometh home, he calleth together his friends and neighbors, saying unto them: Rejoice with me; for I have found my sheep which was lost. I say unto you, that likewise joy shall be in heaven over one sinner that repenteth, more than over ninety and nine just persons which need no repentance. Either what woman having ten pieces of silver, if she lose one piece, doth not light a candle and sweep the house, and seek diligently till she find it? And when she hath found it, she calleth her friends and her neighbors together, saying, Rejoice with me, for I have found the piece which I had lost. Likewise I say unto you, there is joy in the presence of the angels of God over one sinner that repenteth."

Jesus uses these two illustrations not only to establish the fact that there is joy "in heaven over one sinner that repenteth," but also to establish the fact that the rejoicing is done by the friends and the neighbors of the party thus repenting. In both of these illustrations Jesus represents the rejoicing as being done exclusively by the interested parties themselves, and their friends and neighbors. He then declares that the rejoicing in heaven is done "likewise," or in the same manner. This settles the question. Indeed, your own hearts tell you that my views on this subject are correct.

You all cherish a pleasing hope, if not an abiding faith, that after your toils and sorrows of life are past you will join your loved ones in a land of bliss—in the bright abodes where they now dwell. You hope and expect, too, that they will remember you still, and love you as they loved while yet on earth. You hope and expect that your parents will still love you as their child, your children as their father or their mother. Is not all of this true? Do you not also hope and expect that these loved ones will be the first to greet you on the other shore of the great river of death, and to welcome you to their beautiful mansions of fadeless bliss? And would not your anticipated joys of heaven be greatly dimmed if you were to learn that this could never be, that your loved ones would never recognize you again, and that they would feel no more joy upon your arrival among them than they would upon the arrival of a Digger Indian, an Esquimau, or a Hottentot? Do not your own hearts, then, tell you that Spiritualism is a glorious truth, when it teaches that these fond hopes of your yearning hearts are well founded, and that your parents, your children, your loved ones all, with their radiant faces, will, indeed, be the first to come in their robes of snow, on their wings of light, to welcome you to the fadeless joys of their beautiful homes? In order, therefore, that this great joy may exist in heaven, Spiritualism, as you see, is an absolute necessity.

So far as the truth or the nature of Spiritualism is concerned, however, it makes but little difference whether, on any one occasion, the rejoicing in question be done by all the inhabitants of heaven, or only by the friends and the relatives of the particular "sinner that repenteth." If it be done by all, then the friends and the relatives of each penitent are included, and the fact that they all know exactly when to rejoice over the repentance of any particular sinner is proof positive that a constant correspondence is being carried on between our world or condition and their own. The fact, too, that they rejoice at all "over one sinner that repenteth," is proof equally positive that they take a deep interest in the affairs of this world.

Since all these things are true—since our friends in heaven know just what we are doing, and since they so greatly rejoice when any one of us is brought to repentance, can we reasonably doubt that they do all in their power to bring about that repentance? Would they see us go down to eternal ruin without making an effort to save us? Even the rich man in hell tried to save those he loved on earth. And would our friends in heaven do less for us? That they do at least pray for us, we learn from Rev. v, 8, in which we read of four and twenty elders, who minister before the throne of God, and who have "golden vials full of odors, which are the prayers of saints."

These elders are human spirits, representatives of the glorified saints in heaven; and since we cannot reasonably suppose that these glorified saints need longer to offer prayers in their own behalf, we are bound to admit that the prayers which they are offering are in behalf of persons still upon earth. These prayers may proceed directly from saints on earth, or, which is far more likely, from saints in heaven, in behalf of their friends on earth. Be this as it may, however, the prayers, in either case, reach God through the elders, the more perfect of the glorified spirits that minister around his throne.

The doctrine that the saints in heaven do thus receive our prayers, and present them to God, together with their own intercessions in our behalf, always has been held, as an article faith, by the great body of the Christian church. Every Catholic, and every member of the Greek church must believe it; and, although Protestants are not now required to do so, many of them nevertheless do believe it. Its rejection, indeed, for a long time after the so-called Reformation, formed no part of Protestantism. Bitter as he was against the Catholic church, Luther, in regard to this doctrine, was in full harmony with her. He says: "Who can deny that God works great miracles at the tombs of the saints? I, therefore, with the whole Catholic church, hold that the saints are to be honored and invoked by us." In his admonitions to dying persons he says: "Let no one omit to call upon the blessed Virgin and the angels and saints, that they may intercede with God for them at that instant." Many others, also, of the great lights of Protestantism have likewise declared their full belief in this doctrine. Indeed, its truth was never seriously called in question by any considerable number till King Edward's uncle, the Duke of Somerset, and his party, from motives of avarice and ambition, engaged in a relentless war against the Catholic church. For political effect they then rejected this doctrine. They expected, and correctly, too, that after its rejection by themselves, they should be able to render the Catholics odious in the eyes of the ignorant masses, by charging them with idolatry in the invocation of saints. By thus rejecting one of the fundamental, one of the most beautiful and elevating, doctrines of the Bible, and of the Christian church, these self-styled reformers, throughout all Protestantism, sowed the seeds of infidelity which are now bearing abundant harvests.

These arguments then urged by these semi-infidel objectors, and still urged by their semi-infidel followers, against this beautiful doctrine of the communion of saints on earth with saints in heaven, if carried out, would effectually overthrow not only the Catholic church, but also the whole system of Christianity, and, indeed, of every other religion. These men then argued, as you argue now, that since God can, he necessarily does, receive the prayers of his children on earth, directly and in person; and that consequently all those doctrines must necessarily be false and absurd which represent him as receiving them by proxy, or through the agency of saints, of angels, or of any other third parties. Taking up this argument, infidels can very easily prove that, since God can, he necessarily does, make known his will to men directly and in person, and that consequently all those doctrines must, of necessity, be false and absurd which represent him as communicating his will to men by proxy, or through the agency of angels, of prophets, of apostles, of evangelists, of preachers, or of any other third parties. Admitting the correctness of your argument, then, you must see clearly that you have furnished infidelity with a weapon with which it can effectually overthrow the whole fabric of your religion. But is your argument a logical one?

Messages, passing backward and forward between two parties, always are, or at least always may be, conveyed in both directions through the same channel. If, then, it be either improper or impracticable for a message to pass through a certain channel in one direction, it is evidently just as improper or just as impracticable, for one to pass through the same channel in the opposite direction. If, therefore, in teaching that God receives the prayers and other messages of men to himself, through saints, angels, and other third parties, as his agents, the Catholics teach an absurd or an improper doctrine, what kind of a doctrine do you teach, when you represent him as sending all his own messages to men through such third parties? If men can, and do, without the aid of third parties, get their messages all safely through to God, cannot he manage, in the same way, to get his messages all safely through to men?

You teach that God employs legions of angels, and whole armies of prophets, preachers, and other agents, to convey his messages to men. At the same time you teach that he never has these messengers bear back the messages of men to himself. Can these two doctrines be reconciled with each other? Can messengers be necessary in the one direction, and not in the other? Can you advance a single argument in favor of employing agents to bear messages in the one direction, which will not with equal weight bear in favor of employing these same or similar agents to bear messages in the opposite direction? Can you advance a single argument against the employing of messengers in the one direction which will not bear with equal weight against the employing of them in the other? Do not the two doctrines rest upon precisely the same foundation? In rejecting one of them, then, have you not virtually condemned the principle upon which they both equally rest? And does not the condemnation of that principle—the general principle of agency—effectually overturn every known system of religion? Are your teachings, then, anything else than Infidelity in disguise? Are you not aware that, by your teachings and your wranglings, you are doing more to make Infidels than are the writings of all the Paines, the Humes, the Volneys, and the Voltaires that ever lived?

The Bible everywhere teaches that God's dealings with men are almost entirely carried on through agents to whom he delegates the necessary powers. This method of dealing through agents was evidently adopted, not because God needs the aid of any of his creatures, but because just such employment as he gives them is essential to their improvement and happiness; and because, if they were daily to come into direct communication with him, they would inevitably cease to regard him with that awful reverence which is his due. "Familiarity breeds contempt." God could himself have named all the living things which he had made, and could have dressed and kept in order the garden which he had planted, and yet he saw fit to have all of this done by Adam. In one moment of time, and by a mere effort of his will, he could himself have made the ark, and yet he saw fit to have Noah work upon it for one hundred and twenty years. He could himself have known, and he doubtless did know, exactly what the Sodomites were doing on a certain occasion, and yet he saw fit to send messengers to ascertain the facts and report them to him. He could himself have brought all the plagues upon Egypt, he could have divided the waters of the Red Sea, etc., and yet he saw fit to have all these things done by his agent Moses.

When upon Mount Sinai, God could himself have communicated all his commandments and instructions directly to the people, and could in like manner have received directly the people's messages to himself. All these communications, however, as well in the one direction as in the other, he saw fit to have made through his agent Moses, who was kept quite busy sometimes, climbing the mountain to report the people's messages to God, and, at other times, descending it again to report God's messages to the people. When in the wilderness the people cried for water, God could himself have heard, and doubtless did hear, that cry; and yet he saw fit to notice it only when it was reported to him by Moses. Even then, he administered relief only through this same agent.

On many occasions God's anger was so kindled against the children of Israel, because of their rebelliousness, that he threatened to utterly destroy them all. On each of these occasions, however, he saw fit to let himself be persuaded by Moses to forego his contemplated vengeance, and to spare the people. Moses accomplished this persuasion simply by showing him how bad it would look in him to thus fly into a rage, and destroy his own chosen people, whom he had sworn to protect, and by reminding him of what his enemies would say of so rash a proceeding. God suffered himself to be controlled by these arguments, and yet he doubtless understood them as well before they were repeated to him by Moses as he did afterward. It is not at all probable that he really needed either the information which Moses gave him, or the ridicule which Moses cast upon his proposed course of conduct. It is not at all probable that Moses was really the abler reasoner of the two, as on all these occasions he seems to have been. By all this God evidently designed simply to give Moses such exercise and experience as were really necessary to render him what he was destined to become, a mighty reasoner, a wonderful law-giver, a grand model for all nations and for all ages.

When present upon Mount Sinai, God could have

permitted the people to approach him, and to offer in person their prayers, their praises, their sacrifices, etc. Instead of permitting them to do this, however, he threatened them with instant death if they should so much as touch the border of the mountain while he was upon it. Even the priests and the elders were required to remain at a distance. In only a very few instances were any, except Moses, permitted to approach the divine presence. Indeed, the whole history of God's dealings with men goes to prove that, however near he may have been to the people, he has never dealt directly with them, and has never suffered them to deal directly with him. He has always sent his communications to men through agents, and has always required men to send their communications, their prayers, their sacrifices, etc., to him through the same agents. To have borne messages himself in either direction would have constituted him an angel or messenger, and this he has never proposed to be. He requires his creatures to serve him. He never serves them. Were he to come in person after your prayers and other communications, he would be your servant. This you cannot expect him to be.

The people never could present their own prayers, their own sacrifices, etc., in an acceptable manner, and never could make atonement for themselves. On one occasion some of them tried to present their own offerings, and God destroyed them for their sacrilegious presumption. The people always had to bring their offerings, of whatever kind, to one of God's agents or ministers, and have him offer them, in their stead, and thus make atonement for them.

On all these occasions the same priest that presented the people's offerings to God, also, in return, bestowed God's blessing upon the people. In Lev. ix, 7, we read: "And Moses said unto Aaron, Go unto the altar . . . and offer the offering of the people, and make an atonement for them, as the Lord commanded." Aaron did this, and then, as we learn in the twenty-second verse, he "lifted up his hand toward the people, and blessed them." The high priest alone, and he only once a year and after the most thorough purifications, was permitted to enter into the immediate presence of God in the most holy place.

Before God, the prophets, the priests, and other agents, stood as the representatives of the people, and in that capacity they offered to God the petitions of the people, their sacrifices, etc., and did all other things which the people themselves would have done had they been permitted to act in person. Before the people these same agents stood as the representatives of God himself, and in that capacity they proclaimed God's will to the people, made known his promises, threatened them with his judgments, imposed his penalties, or bestowed his blessings upon them, pardoned their sins, and did all other things which God himself would have done had he seen fit to act in person.

All these things are so clearly taught in the Bible that from me they require no further illustration. The only question now is: Has God ever ceased to deal thus with men, through agents, and come to deal with them in person, as a man deals with his fellow-men? To this question no intelligent person can give other than a negative answer. Since the principles which govern God's actions can never be outside of himself—since they form, so to speak, a part of his own being—they must, of necessity, be as unchangeable as his own nature. Hence it follows that his method of dealing with men, through agents, though it may have been changed in form to suit the changed conditions of men, can never have been changed in principle. As well might you assert that his method of governing the material universe by fixed laws, by physical forces, has been changed for some other method. To assert a change in the principle of his government is simply to assert a change in his own character. And dare you assert any such change as this?

You teach correctly that God still communicates his word to men through agents, just as he did four thousand years ago. You teach correctly that millions of Bibles and thousands of preachers are necessary in order that all men may receive that word. And yet, while you teach that all these agents are necessary to convey God's word to men, you absurdly teach that no agents at all are necessary to convey men's word to God; that men can, and do, in person hand in their own prayers and other communications directly to God himself. But is God everywhere to hear, and nowhere to speak? Do not exactly the same space and the same obstacles intervene between men and God as intervene between God and men? If, then, men can speak directly through this space and these obstacles to God, cannot he do the same to them? Do not the communications from the one side require for their transmittal precisely the same means as are required by those from the other side? Are they not all conveyed, then, by one and the same grand and indivisible system of communication? What would you think of a government which should, at great expense to the people, provide thousands of mails to carry letters, papers, etc., in one direction, but which would not permit these mails to carry anything at all in the opposite direction? And do you not blasphemously represent God as acting in this absurd manner? If messengers between God and men are necessary at all, are they not bound to be equally necessary in both directions? If such messengers are not necessary at all, are not your prophets, your preachers, etc., all shameless impostors, and your churches monstrous swindles?

If the system of agency which we are considering be designed, not as a necessity, but merely as a means of giving elevating employment, for the benefit of those engaged in it, would not the benefit be as great in carrying prayers, etc., from men to God as it is in carrying commandments, etc., from God to men? Wherein, then, is the difference? Simply in the pay. If the conveying of men's prayers, etc., to God paid as many priests, and paid them as well, as does the conveying of God's word to men, does any one doubt that there would be just as much of it done? In that case, would there not be just as much need of messengers to God as there now is for messengers from him?

Be all this as it may, however, Jesus testifies in the most positive manner that God's method of carrying on his government through agents was continued unchanged, from the Jewish into the Christian Dispensation, and that it is to continue unchanged during all time on earth, and during all eternity in heaven. For all the intercommunications between the spirit world and our own, then, the agency of spirits is necessary, and Spiritualism is still, as it always has been, the grand medium through which God's government is carried on.

In the first place, it is to be observed that, while in the body, Jesus never acted in any but his human character. Had he acted in his divine character, his example would have been totally worthless to us, since none of us aspire to godship, and since none of us could ever hope to imitate God, much less to equal or to surpass him. Every act of Jesus was the act of a man, and was intended as a model for us, not only to imitate but to equal and even to surpass. While astonishing the people with his works, Jesus says: "Verily, verily, I say unto you, He that believeth on me, the works that I do shall he do also; and greater works than these shall he do." This declaration he substantially repeats on several occasions, and then, in his last earthly meeting with his disciples, he commands them not only to do these works themselves, but also to teach all nations to do them, and promises that in the doing of these works he will be with " them that believe," "alway, even unto the end of the world."

Jesus also emphatically disclaims the possession of any power not delegated to him by God the father. In John v, 19, 20, he says: "Verily, verily, I say unto you, the son can do nothing of himself, but what he seeth the father do: for what things soever he doeth, these also doeth the son likewise.

For the father loveth the son, and showeth him all the things that himself doeth; and he will show him greater works than these that ye may marvel." In the twenty-second verse he says: "For the father judgeth no man, but hath committed all judgment to the son." In Luke x, 22, he says: "All things are delivered unto me of my father."

Thus you see how full were the powers which God bestowed upon Jesus, and which Jesus, in turn, bestowed upon "them that believe." These powers enabled their possessors to heal diseases, to cast out devils, to pardon sins, to raise the dead, to commune with spirits, and to do all other things which Jesus himself, their model, in his human character had been accustomed to do. Since all his acts were meant to be models for men, none of them required greater powers than are delegated to men. Indeed, as I have already quoted, he bestowed upon the true believer power to do even "greater works than these." If, therefore, you hear that some one is performing greater works than were ever performed by Jesus, do not rashly condemn the report until you have given the matter a fair investigation. If Jesus spoke the truth, such works must be done. He does not say that such works may possibly be done by some unknown believer in some remote corner of the globe, but emphatically declares that such works "shall" be done by the true believer, whoever he may be, whenever he may live, and in whatever country. If, then, your neighbors, Mr. Smith, Mr. Brown, Mr. Jones, and others, be true believers, they are sure to be doing some of the works which as "signs shall follow them that believe." They are sure to be healing the sick, speaking in unknown tongues, communing with spirits, etc., and, very probably, in consequence of these works, they may be also raising the devil among the church-going people of the neighborhood. If you do not like to have such things going on in your vicinity, all you have to do is either to move away into some neighborhood in which there are no true believers, or else pitch into Jesus, who brought it about that these "signs shall" inevitably "follow them that believe."

In Luke x, 16, on sending out these seventy disciples, Jesus says: "He that heareth you, heareth me; and he that despiseth you, despiseth me; and he that despiseth me, despiseth him that sent me." On several other occasions he substantially repeats these same declarations. From all this you see how fully the true minister of the gospel is empowered to act as the representative of Jesus, and through him as the representative of God himself.

In Matt. x, 20, Jesus says: "For it is not ye that speak, but the spirit of your father, which speaketh in you." The apostles, then, were simply speaking mediums. In the eighth verse of the same chapter Jesus commands these mediums to "heal the sick, cleanse the lepers, raise the dead, cast out devils; freely ye have received, freely give." From this we learn that the apostles were developed in all the various phases of spiritual mediumship. You will also notice that the instructions given on this occasion are not merely permissory, but are mandatory. The apostles not only may, and can, but absolutely must perform all these works. Among many other things, they all must "raise the dead." But how could they "raise the dead" without calling back the spirits of the dead from the abodes to which they had gone in the spirit world? And would not such a calling back of the spirits of the dead be a phase of pure Spiritualism? Does not Jesus, then, command Spiritualism to be practiced by "them that believe," "alway, even unto the end of the world?" And has this command to "raise the dead" ever been fulfilled? I contend that it has; not in the two or three instances in which the apostles are said to have resuscitated the bodies of apparently dead persons, but in the millions of instances in which Spiritualists and others of "them that believe" have raised the dead in the form of spirits.

If, however, by the raising of the dead we are to understand the resuscitating of absolutely dead bodies, then the command never has been, never can be, and consequently never will be fulfilled. In that case the giving of such a command was a downright absurdity. Jesus knew very well that the revivifying of such bodies was rarely, if ever, within the limits of possibility. And would he, knowing this, have bound such an impossibility, as an unavoidable duty, upon all the apostles, and, through them, upon all the nations of the world?

You claim that the command in question was fulfilled by one or two of the apostles, in the revivifying of two or three dead bodies. As well might you claim that the commands to heal the sick, to cleanse the lepers, to cast out devils, and to preach the gospel, were all fulfilled by one or two of the apostles in the healing of two or three sick persons, the cleansing of two or three lepers, the casting out of two or three devils, and the preaching of the gospel to two or three persons. According to your teachings the whole commission given by Jesus was fulfilled by the works of two or three of the apostles. What a farce, then, you make of Christianity! Did not Jesus, in all cases, inseparably connect the doing of these works with the preaching of the gospel? Without fear of successful contradiction, I contend that he did, and that every man is an impostor who pretends to preach the gospel, without being endued with power from on high to do these works. Were not these works the things that Jesus principally dwelt upon when sending out the apostles? Were not these works, as well as the gospel which they were to accompany, to be blessings to all nations and to all ages? And was the revivifying of two or three dead bodies, in Judea, and the causing of them again to suffer the pangs of death, any great blessing to all nations and to all ages? So of the healing of two or three sick persons, the cleansing of two or three lepers, etc. Would these things be of any special benefit to the balance of mankind? Did not Jesus foresee all things? If he did, and if he foresaw that, in all future ages, only two or three dead persons ever could be, or ever would be, raised from the dead, would he, think you, have so frequently, and so earnestly, enjoined the raising of the dead, as a duty, upon all his followers of all nations and of all ages? Would these few cases have been of so vast importance as to be incorporated, as an essential element, into the system of religion which he was founding? And did Jesus, in the distribution of his favors, propose to be unjust and partial? Did he have in view two or three special favorites whom he proposed to have raised from the dead, while he left all the other dead to crumble into dust? Am I under any obligation to love or to praise him for having some unknown Jew raised from the dead eighteen hundred years ago, when he will have nothing of the kind done for my own child, the light of my own home, whose cold form lies before me? What kind of a being do you make of him by your absurd infidel teachings?

The death and the decay of the body are inevitable processes of nature, and Jesus never made it a duty to undo what nature, in her legitimate action, has done. He never meant that we should raise up or revivify bodies once absolutely dead. "It is appointed to men once to die," says Paul. Your view of the doctrine of raising the dead would make them die more than once. By raising a man from the dead every time he died we might make him die a thousand deaths, and there is nothing more to hinder us from raising him a second, a third, or a thousandth time, than there is to hinder us from raising him the first time. And do you think that many persons, and especially the righteous, when once in the spirit world, would regard it as any great favor to be called back to again inhabit their old body, so full of infirmities, and to be subjected a second time to the agonies of death? Is it not evident, then, that, by the raising of the dead, Jesus means the calling up of spirits—the bringing into communion of the saints on earth with the saints in heaven? And does this not make Spiritualism the most glorious element in the Christian religion?

In Matt. xvi, 18, 19, Jesus says: "And I say also unto thee that thou art Peter, and upon this rock I will build my church, and the gates of hell shall not prevail against it. And I will give unto thee the keys of the kingdom of heaven: and whatsoever thou shalt bind on earth, shall be bound in heaven, and whatever thou shalt loose on earth, shall be loosed in heaven." In another place he gives to all of his disciples this same power to bind and to loose things on earth and in heaven. From this we learn that, both on earth and in heaven, God's government was still to be conducted on the principle of agency. As God's agents, the apostles were to exercise a certain amount of authority in both worlds; and in order that they might be able to do this—in order that the binding and the loosing might be carried on simultaneously in both—it was evidently necessary that there should be a constant correspondence carried on between the two worlds. The carrying on of this correspondence again renders Spiritualism an absolute necessity in God's general government.

In John xx, 21–23, we read: "Then said Jesus unto them again, Peace be unto you: as my father hath sent me, even so send I you. And when he had said this he breathed on them, and said unto them, Receive ye the Holy Ghost; Whosesoever sins ye remit, they are remitted unto them; and whosesoever sins ye retain, they are retained." From this we learn that in receiving the Holy Ghost the apostles came into possession of the very same power by which Jesus himself had performed all his wonderful works. This power, as we have already seen, enabled them to heal the sick, to raise the dead, to commune with spirits, to pardon sins, and to do all the other works which Jesus did, and even "greater works than these."

And now the question arises: Did the apostles receive these powers, and the duties which accompanied them, in their individual, or in their representative, capacities? If in their individual capacities, then, of course, at their death, all these powers necessarily ceased; and with them, of course, also ceased all those duties, including the preaching of the gospel, which were expressly founded on these powers, and which were never required, and never authorized to be performed by any to whom these powers were wanting. If, in his individual capacity, Peter was made the foundation of the church, and the possessor of the keys of the kingdom of heaven, then it follows that at his death the church, for want of a foundation, necessarily fell; and that the keys of the kingdom of heaven were lost, or, at least, rendered utterly useless, for want of some one to hold them.

If all this be true, and it must be according to your own teachings, then it is evident that the Christian church ceased to exist 1800 years ago, and that ever since the death of Peter the gates of the kingdom of heaven have remained just as he left them, open to all, or closed to all, without any distinction whatever. No Protestant dares name Peter's successor. Thus you see that, by your own teachings, you are left without any church at all, and without any hope of salvation, unless you propose to steal into heaven through the gates left unguarded by the death of Peter, and the loss of his keys.

If, however, as Jesus plainly teaches, Peter and the other apostles received their powers and their instructions in their representative or official capacities, then, of course, those powers and instructions would be transmitted, unimpaired, to their successors in office. In this case the Christian church still remains firm as the rock on which it was founded, "and the gates of hell shall not prevail against it." In this case, too, remain, of course, unimpaired both the power and the duty to heal the sick, to raise the dead—by calling up spirits—to cast out devils, to preach the gospel, to pardon sins, and to do all the other works which Jesus commanded. In other words, both the power and the duty remain to practice every phase of Spiritualism.

But do you possess the powers which were conferred upon the apostles and their successors? You admit that you do not. And without possessing any of their powers can you perform any of their duties? Were the duties ever separate from the powers? If not, what are you, what can you be, but detected impostors? You are forced to the disagreeable alternative of either denying the existence of any true church at all, or of admitting that your hated rivals are that church. In either case you inevitably reduce to a set of barefaced pretenders.

In Matt. xix, 28, we read: "And Jesus said unto them, Verily, verily, I say unto you that ye which have followed me in the regeneration, when the son of man shall sit in the throne of his glory, ye also shall sit upon twelve thrones judging the twelve tribes of Israel." In Luke xxii, 29, 30, we have this same promise in different words: "And I appoint unto you a kingdom, as my father hath appointed unto me; that ye may eat and drink at my table in my kingdom, and sit on thrones judging the twelve tribes of Israel." This promise was made in reply to Peter, who wished to know what he and the other disciples were to receive in exchange for the houses, the fish-nets, and the other property which they had been compelled to abandon in order to follow Jesus.

In making this promise Jesus either meant what he said, or else he meant to cruelly deceive the simple-minded and confiding men to whom he made it. They certainly understood the kingdoms, the thrones, etc., promised to them, to be just as real as were the houses, the fish nets, etc., given in exchange. Jesus knew very well how they understood his promise, and yet, so far from correcting that understanding, as he certainly should have done, had it been an erroneous one, he confirmed it on several occasions. If, then, Jesus was not a deceiver, we have in this matter the most positive evidence that in heaven as well as on earth God's government is carried on by men whom he appoints as his agents or representatives. You are bound to admit that, if Jesus spoke the truth, the twelve apostles actually do, at this present time, "sit upon twelve thrones judging the twelve tribes of Israel."

It is an undeniable fact that in his dealings with men God is governed by his desire for their improvement and their happiness. It is also an equally undeniable fact that, without a change in God's own nature, there can be no change in that desire, or in the actions which proceed from it. But how does God promote the improvement and the happiness of men? Simply by giving them ennobling and happifying employments. In what other way could he render them either better or happier? And what could be more ennobling, what could render us more supremely happy, than to be constantly engaged in doing God's work, in helping to carry on his government, in laboring for the improvement of our fellow-men in time, and for their happiness in eternity. Hence it is that in both worlds God has countless numbers of men acting as teachers, as judges, etc., while he has millions of others acting as messengers, or angels, between the two worlds. Indeed, in his goodness and wisdom, God has given us all, whether in the body or out of it, something to do, if we will, for our own improvement, in the carrying on of his general government. Take from good men all those ennobling employments which in this life God gives them, and on what would then depend their further improvement, and their continued happiness? And if such employments are so necessary to our improvement and happiness in this life, can they be less necessary in the world of spirits? Is there, beyond the change called death, no such thing as further improvement? And does death deprive a good man of all that unselfish love of his kind which renders him so god-like while yet on earth? Does his entrance into heaven drive from his soul all desire for the well-being of his loved ones on earth—all willingness to labor, or even to pray, for their salvation?

For forty long years, without any hope of earthly reward, Moses labored and suffered for his ungrateful and rebellious people. On several occasions, as we have already seen, his interpositions alone saved them from utter destruction at the hands of their offended God. On more than one occasion, too, God offered to make of him a greater and mightier people than were they. Moses, however, loving his people more than he loved himself, prayed God to spare them, or to let him perish with them. The last days on earth of this wonderful man were spent in giving warnings and instructions to his people, and in prayers to God for their welfare. And dare you deliberately assert that his entrance into heaven robbed his great heart of all that wonderful depth of love and solicitude which he felt for them while yet on earth? Dare you deliberately assert that he nevermore cared what befell them, and that he never again interceded for them at the throne of the God he loved? And dare you deliberately assert that such intercessions, if made, were of no avail? Would God heed them when coming from Moses, a man on earth, and then despise them when coming from Moses, a glorified saint in heaven?

I might also ask these same questions in regard to that other equally wonderful man, the prophet Elijah. After reading of all that he did, and of all that he suffered, for his people, dare you deliberately assert that by his translation into heaven without undergoing the change called death he lost all love for his people, and all desire for their well-being?

When, upon the mount of transfiguration, Jesus met Moses and Elijah, did he find them both totally destitute of all interest in the welfare of those for whose salvation himself was then about to die? Would he, at so solemn a time, have sought an interview with them if they had been thus cold, thus heartless, thus totally dead to all the god-like emotions which were then welling up in his own great bosom? When on earth, were they not very much like Jesus? And would the influences surrounding them in heaven cause them to thus degenerate and to become so unlike him? If not, would not these two great men, these two renowned spirits, still labor and pray for the welfare of the inhabitants of earth?

You believe that it is right for good men on earth to labor and to pray for the salvation of those they love. You believe that they neglect a great duty when they fail so to do. Can it be wrong, then, for these same men to do these same things in a more perfect manner after they have become saints in heaven? And would they not, in their glorified state, have more leisure for these works of love than they had when burdened with the toils and cares of life in their earthly condition?

You believe that it is right for us to ask the prayers of good men on earth. Can it be wrong, then, to ask the more perfect prayers of these same men or of others after they have become glorified saints in heaven? If it be idolatry, as you teach that it is, to invoke the interposition of the saints and the angels in heaven, are you not guilty of practicing a much lower form of idolatry in invoking the intercession of your poor erring friends upon earth? Can it be right to invoke the aid of a lower being, and wrong to invoke the aid of a higher? If so, then, of course, the lower the being or the object is that we invoke, the better is our act; and, conversely, the higher the being is that we invoke, the worse is our act. On this principle those pagans who worship monkeys, serpents, etc., are wiser and better than you are, who worship the most high God himself.

But can a doctrine be true which involves absurdities so monstrous? If it be right, as you teach that it is, to invoke the aid of God, the highest, and of man, the lowest, of intelligent beings, how can it be wrong to invoke the aid of saints, of angels, or of any other intermediate order of beings? Can saints and angels be too high, when we are invoking a being still higher? Can they be too low, when we are invoking a being still lower? You invoke the two extremes, but does safety usually lie in the extremes, or between them?

Sinners are like sailors clinging to a wreck that is fast going to pieces upon the rocks. And since, to sailors thus situated, it is right to invoke the aid of anything, from a water spaniel to the grandest monarch of earth, it cannot be wrong in the sinner to invoke the aid of any good being, from the lowest savage to the highest God.

You teach that God hears the imperfect prayers of men on earth in behalf of those they love. At your revival meetings you call upon all those persons to come forward who desire an interest in the prayers of those whom, from some unaccountable freak of fancy, you are pleased to style "God's people." And God either does or does not hear such prayers. If he does not hear them, then your teachings are false, your revival meetings are frauds, and yourselves are impostors. If he does hear them, then it devolves upon you to prove that he does not, with equal favor, hear the more perfect prayers of the saints and the angels in heaven, in behalf of those they love. Is he more pleased with prayers coming from the less pure and the less perfect of his children than he is with similar prayers coming from the more pure and the more perfect? If he is, then the more impure and the more imperfect you are, the more certain you are of his favor. It may be from this view of the subject that some of you feel so sure of reaching heaven. On what other ground can you claim that God rejects the pure and perfect prayers of the holy Virgin, of the apostles, of the martyrs, of the angels, and of the archangels, and yet receives the miserable balderdash which you offer up in the form of prayer, from very imperfect hearts, and which is often wafted to his ear on breath foul from undigested food, from unwashed teeth, and from the nauseous fumes of cheap tobacco? Do you see nothing monstrous, nothing blasphemous, in your doctrine that God's actions can be and are influenced by these prayers of yours, while he is utterly impervious to the prayers of the countless millions of glorified beings who surround his throne?

Not long ago four young children stood weeping by the bedside of their dying mother. Amid their sobs they were listening to her faintly whispered words, as, for the last time on earth, she prayed God to bless and to protect them. Having in turn prayed for each of the eldest three, she placed her wasted hand upon the little curly head of her youngest, a bright, sweet child of only five summers, and whispered, "Johnnie, my poor, dear child, mamma must leave you, but may God——" Here her words ceased. Her lifeless hand dropped from his head.

Her spirit had gone to him who gave it. The child, perceiving that she did not proceed, and having a vague sense of the terrible calamity that had fallen upon him, cried: "O mamma! mamma! pray for me, too! pray for me, too!" His invocation was to the dead, to a disembodied spirit, to a glorified saint in heaven. And dare you, because of this invocation, stigmatize that innocent child as an idolater? Was it not just as right, and just as proper, for him to invoke his mother's intercession, a moment after her change, as it was a moment before? And was it not just as right, and just as proper, for that mother to finish her prayer in his behalf as a glorified saint in heaven as it was for her to begin it as a poor, suffering mortal on earth? Can that which is right and proper in an erring mortal be wrong and immoral in a glorified spirit? If not, would not that mother be sure to finish in heaven the prayer for her child which she had begun upon earth? And dare you assert that the last part of that prayer, if offered, was not as acceptable to God as was the first?

Finally, our friends in heaven, of necessity, either do know our affairs, and take an interest in them, or they do not. They either do rejoice "over one sinner that repenteth," or they do not. They either do aid us with their prayers, and their angelic ministrations, or they do not. If they do all these things, then is Spiritualism unquestionably a grand, a glorious reality, an absolute necessity in the wonderfully sublime workings of the government of God. Then, in the eloquent language of a Milner, "We hold daily and hourly converse, to our unspeakable comfort and advantage, with the angelic choirs, with the venerable patriarchs and prophets of ancient times, with the heroes of Christianity, the blessed apostles and martyrs, and with the bright ornaments of its later ages, the Bernards, the Xaviers, the Tereses, and the Saleses," and, as he might with equal truth have added, with our parents, our brothers, our sisters, our children, our loved ones all—changed and glorified in their forms and their conditions, but no less our friends, no less our kindred, no less fondly treasured in our hearts, now than they were in the days departed, when they were the joys and the lights of our earthly homes.

If, however, after entering heaven, our friends never again labor, or even pray, for us, then their failure to do so must, of necessity, be either because they have lost all desire for our salvation, or else because they have lost all liberty to do anything that might tend to save us. There can be no other possible reason. If they retained both the desire and the liberty to labor and to pray for us, would they not be sure to do so? Which have they lost, then, their desire for our salvation, or their liberty to even pray for it?

If, the moment they enter heaven, our friends cease to care whether we are saved or damned, what do they become? Cold, heartless, loveless, emotionless, and, necessarily, joyless beings. Indeed, they become worse than the rich man in hell, since he still loved his brethren on earth, and prayed that warning might be sent them, lest they, too, should come to his place of torment. And dare you assert that our parents, our children, our dear ones all, on entering heaven, universally cease to love us, and to pray for us, when even this damned spirit in hell still continued to love his friends on earth, and to do all he could to save them?

Do you who are parents believe that on entering heaven you will lose all love for your children, and all desire for their salvation? If, by praying for them, you could save them, or even hope to save them, from the unutterable torments of an endless hell, and to have them join you amid the fadeless joys, the untold glories, of your world of light, would you not continue to pray for them just as earnestly as you ever prayed for them on earth? Your own hearts tell you that you would. You know that God's love, shed abroad in your hearts, even in this world of toil and of sorrow, makes you love your children more than ever, and more than ever desire that they may turn to God, and share with you the blissful hope of eternal happiness. And will not God's still greater love shed abroad in your hearts, will not the still greater joys of heaven itself, still heighten your love for your children, and your desire for their eternal salvation? Your own fond hearts tell you that they will. The desire, then, to labor and to pray for the salvation of their friends on earth does not forsake those who enter heaven. If, therefore, they do not thus labor and pray, it must, of necessity, be because God prohibits them to engage in such labors of love. But dare you bring so blasphemous an accusation against God? Dare you, after a moment's thought, assert that he turns legions of devils loose to lead our loved ones to eternal ruin, while at the same time he will not permit us, after entering heaven, to even pray for those loved ones thus endangered? This is certainly what you thoughtlessly teach. It is the very essence of Protestant orthodoxy. But does it not make God a worse being than the devil himself? And does it not necessarily render heaven a place of indescribable torment?

Thus you see that if you have our spirit friends of choice cease their labors of love for us, you make them worse than the damned; if you have them cease these labors through compulsion, you make God worse than the devil; and if you do not have them cease these labors at all, you make Spiritualism a grand, a glorious truth, an absolute necessity in the government of God. And now, what will you do?

In Luke v, 22, we read: "For the father judgeth no man, but hath committed all judgment unto the son." From this we learn that Jesus is the supreme judge of the living and of the dead. To him is committed "all judgment," no matter where, and no matter concerning whom that judgment is to be exercised. This unlimited power of judgment constitutes him, in reality, a king, and so he evidently regards it, since he often speaks of his throne and of his kingdom. Say what we may, then, of the superiority of republican institutions, we find nothing resembling them in the government of heaven. The founders of that government were certainly uncompromising monarchists, and the government itself is certainly an absolute monarchy or despotism, to which we must uncomplainingly submit, should we ever in the mutations of time come under the jurisdiction of that government at all.

Be all this as it may, however, Jesus, as I have already elsewhere quoted, says unto his disciples: "And I appoint unto you a kingdom, as my father hath appointed unto me; that . . . ye may sit on thrones judging the twelve tribes of Israel." From this we learn that sufficient power to constitute each of them a king is delegated by Jesus to certain human spirits, whom he associates with himself in the grand work of governing his universal kingdom. These associate judges, therefore, or subaltern kings, must necessarily differ in their conditions and their occupations from the less distinguished inhabitants of heaven. Their conditions and their occupations must, of necessity, correspond to the dignity of the offices to which they have been appointed. For obvious reasons many persons are pleased to believe that in heaven the most incorrigible fool becomes at once the equal of the most distinguished philosopher. From what we have just seen, however, this doctrine is a very fallacious one. Indeed, the Bible everywhere teaches that there are various grades among the inhabitants of heaven. Those persons, then, who are content to be fools on earth need not hope to be miraculously made philosophers in heaven. "As the tree falleth, so it lieth." The fool on earth will be a fool in heaven.

In order to be "judging the twelve tribes of Israel," or any other divisions of the inhabitants of God's government, the judges must, of necessity, be actually hearing and deciding the causes which arise among those over whom they preside. Being associated with Jesus in this work, and acting under his authority, their mode of judging cannot be different from his own. Indeed, in this respect they stand in exactly the same relation to him from whom they derive their kingdoms and their powers that he stands in relation to God the father, from whom he derives his kingdom and his powers. Throughout the whole universal government there must, of necessity, be the most perfect harmony of action. In whatever way, then, Jesus is himself occupied, those also must be occupied to whom he assigns a portion of his own work. If, as supreme judge, he takes cognizance of human affairs, and makes intercession for men with the father, these associate judges, engaged in the same work, must, of necessity, do the same, or must at least intercede with him, as he intercedes with the father. In order to do this they must, of equal necessity, have a thorough knowledge of men and of all their affairs; and the possession of such knowledge on their part involves the necessity of a constant correspondence between the inhabitants of earth and those of heaven. In any view of the case, therefore, Spiritualism again becomes a grand and glorious truth, an absolute necessity in God's general government.

In order to escape this conclusion, however, you resort to the totally groundless assumption that the thrones, the kingdoms, the dignified occupations of judging, etc., are merely figurative thrones, figurative kingdoms, figurative occupations, etc., which never had any existence in reality. By this subterfuge you do, indeed, escape your present difficulty, but you thereby fall into a much greater one, since you thus make Jesus a liar and a cheat, and equally reduce his throne, his kingdom, and his occupation of judging to mere figures of speech.

As I have already shown, these thrones, these kingdoms, these dignified occupations, etc., were promised by Jesus to his most faithful followers, not only as rewards of merit, but also as remuneration for real time spent in his service, and in return for real property—houses, fishing tackle, etc., abandoned by his order. For these real services, these various kinds of real property, the followers of Jesus desired, and justly expected, something equally real in return, and when they asked what this was to be, Jesus, in the language which I have quoted, declared that to his chosen twelve it was to be a throne and a kingdom to each, and the dignified occupation of judging one of the twelve tribes of Israel. To his other followers he made this general promise: "And every-one that hath forsaken houses, or brethren, or sisters, or father, or mother, or wife, or children, or lands, for my name's sake, shall receive a hundred-fold, and shall inherit eternal life."

And now, let me ask, in what do these thrones, these kingdoms, this hundredfold, etc., promised in return for real property, consist? They certainly cannot consist merely in eternal life, since this, as you see, is distinctly promised in addition to all of them. Of necessity, therefore, they must consist in something that forms no part of eternal life. What, then, could they have been? You will doubtless admit that Jesus made, at least, a respectable use of language. If you be a grammarian, you will also admit that no respectable speaker or writer ever intermixes real objects and figurative objects in the same sentence, and in the same connection; that no one ever puts real wine into figurative bottles, or figurative wine into real bottles. So of the things in question. You must admit that Jesus could not make real men sit upon figurative thrones, nor have real people judged by figurative judges. If, then, the apostles were real men, and the twelve tribes of Israel were real people, then the thrones, the kingdoms, etc., mentioned in the same sentence, and in the same connection, are bound to be equally real objects. So of the hundredfold promised in return for the lands, the houses, etc., abandoned for the service of Jesus. If the onefold abandoned was real, the hundredfold promised are bound to be equally real. The nature of a quantity is never changed by multiplication. Every mathematician knows that the product is always composed of the same kind of units as is the multiplicand. When Jesus, therefore, for a multiplicand, takes a certain concrete quantity, composed of houses, lands, etc., and multiplies it by one hundred, what does he obtain for a product? What could he obtain but a hundred times as many houses, a hundred times as much land, etc., as were represented in the multiplicand? Could he in this operation, by any possibility, obtain for a product a figurative or imaginary quantity?

To give the language in question any other than a literal meaning is simply to change it into disgusting nonsense. To give it any other meaning would also be to make Jesus an unmitigated scoundrel, since it would make him, by a wilful abuse of language, deceive his trusting and faithful followers, and thus evade the payment of any portion of that which he solemnly promised them, when they entered his service, and to which they were so justly entitled.

Suppose that a wealthy and powerful earthly monarch, about to engage in a great war, should by solemn proclamation promise that to each one of his subjects who would enlist in his army, and serve faithfully until honorably discharged, he would pay a liberal sum each month as wages, and would, in addition to this, at the close of the war, pay each soldier a specified sum of money as bounty, and give him a specified amount of land; and would, in addition to all these things, pay full value for all the property which anyone might have to abandon in order to enter his service. Suppose, further, that, loving their monarch, and trusting implicitly in his promises, thousands of his subjects should leave their all, as did Peter and others in the case of Jesus, and should rally to his standard, and through countless toils, dangers, and sufferings, should win for him the victory. Suppose still further that at the close of the war this monarch should have in his treasury untold sums of money, which he could himself never use, and within his domains millions of square miles of vacant lands, which he could himself never occupy. Suppose, finally, that when his war-worn veterans returned he should refuse to pay them anything at all; and, to excuse his damnable perfidy, should coolly inform them that the money and the lands which he had promised them were figurative money and figurative lands. What would you think of such a monarch? And yet, do you not by your blasphemous teachings represent Jesus as acting in this unspeakably odious manner?

Besides all this, your teachings make eternal life a mere figure of speech, and not a reality. It is mentioned as one of the items in the list of things promised by Jesus on this occasion. It and the other items are all promised in answer to the same question, and in exactly the same sense. If, therefore, the thrones, the kingdoms, etc., mentioned at the same time, and in the same connection, be merely figurative objects, never to be possessed in reality, the same is bound to be equally true of eternal life. The objects promised by Jesus on this occasion are all equally real in themselves, and, being all mentioned in the same connection, and in the same sense, they must, of necessity, as mentioned here, be all equally real, or all equally unreal. You have no right, therefore, to go through the list as you have gone, and select certain items, according as they suit you, to be real, and certain others to be figurative. You must accept the entire list as real, or reject it as unreal. What would Peter and the other disciples have thought if, in answer to their question as to what they should have for all they had forsaken to follow him, Jesus had replied that in reality they were to have nothing at all, but that figuratively they were to have thrones, kingdoms, etc., and were to be engaged in the dignified occupation of "judging the twelve tribes of Israel?" So of the lands, the houses, eternal life, etc. ; if they were all merely figurative rewards, never to be possessed in reality, what advantage could they have ever been to those to whom they were promised, and what would those parties have thought if, when making this promise, Jesus had informed them that he was speaking figuratively, and that in reality he would never give them anything at all?

According to your teachings, the throne, the kingdom, and the occupation of Jesus become like those of the apostles, merely figurative objects which have no real existence. He positively declares: "And I appoint unto you a kingdom, as my father hath appointed unto me." In order that his appointment unto them might be made as was his father's appointment unto him, it was absolutely necessary, as every grammarian knows, that the two appointments should be made in exactly the same manner, and in exactly the same sense. By substituting these two phrases, therefore, for the word as in the text, we have the exact meaning fully and clearly expressed. "And I appoint unto you a kingdom, in the same manner and in the same sense that my father hath appointed unto me." These same remarks apply also with equal force to the occupation of judging which was to accompany these several kingdoms. In the same manner and in the same sense in which the father hath committed all judgment unto the son, the latter, in turn, hath recommitted a portion of it to the apostles and others whom, as we have already seen, he hath associated with himself in the grand work of carrying on his universal government. If, then, all those things which he hath committed to these persons be unreal, so, of necessity, must all those be which his father hath appointed unto himself. These appointments all rest on exactly the same authority, and are spoken of in exactly the same sense. Of necessity, then, they must all be equally real, or all equally unreal. If they be all real, then is Spiritualism bound to be real, too, and to be an absolute necessity in the conducting of the government of God. If, however, they be all unreal, then, of necessity, religion is bound to be a mere farce, heaven a mere fiction, the church a monstrous swindle, and yourselves the most unscrupulous of impostors. You cannot deny the justness of my conclusions, and now you may choose which horn of this dilemma you will take. Choose which you may, your cause is irretrievably lost.

In the sixteenth chapter of Luke we have quite a spicy dialogue carried on between the patriarch Abraham and the rich man, whom I have already mentioned as being in hell. From this dialogue, and from what precedes it, we obtain much valuable information bearing upon our subject. From the fact that Lazarus was borne by angels to Abraham's bosom, we learn that the spirits of the righteous are not conveyed to the place of their future abode by the direct power of God, but by finite beings to whom this work is assigned. As I fully proved in my first lecture, many, if not all, of the angels of heaven are human spirits. In that same lecture I also proved that, whether they be angels themselves or not, "the spirits of just men made perfect" "are as the angels which are in heaven," and "equal unto them." In order that they may thus be "as the angels which are in heaven," and "equal unto" them, it is absolutely necessary that these spirits be surrounded by the same conditions, engaged in the same occupations, and possessed of the same degree of power as are the angels. Whatever, then, may be the conditions, the occupations, and the powers of angels, the same are bound to be the conditions, the occupations, and the powers of "the spirits of just men made perfect." In the case before us, therefore, we have positive evidence, not only that human spirits have work assigned them, but also that upon errands, such as the bearing away of new-born spirits, they pass freely backward and forward between earth and heaven. And all this proves conclusively, not only the truth, but also the heaven-approved, the heaven-necessary, character of Spiritualism.

From the fact that the rich man in hell and Abraham in heaven were distinctly visible to each other, and from the fact that they carried on with each other a direct conversation, we learn that their respective places of abode cannot be very far apart. If, then, as you teach, heaven is up, in what direction is hell, how far are the two places apart, and how far are they both from where we now are?

From the fact that, instead of praying directly to God, the rich man prayed to a human spirit, we learn that, in the opinion of the petitioner at least, this was the surest method of obtaining relief. You may object that the unfortunate circumstance of his being in hell so injured this damned man's reputation as to render his opinions and his testimony comparatively worthless. This, however, does not by any means follow. On the contrary, the fact of his being in hell gives additional weight both to his opinions and his testimony. We all admit that God never makes a fool and then damns him. The fact, then, that this man had been damned effectually establishes his intelligence—a very important qualification in a witness. Besides this, since we cannot doubt the sincerity of one who, from out the midst of flames, cries for water or for other relief, we are bound to admit that the unfortunate circumstance of his being in hell effectually establishes this man's sincerity—the most important of all the qualifications of a witness. Situated as he was, he would certainly appeal to what he sincerely believed to be the proper authority. If hell-fire cannot make a man earnest and sincere in his prayers, what can? The testimony before us, then, is that of an intelligent and sincere man; of a man, too, who belonged to the wealthy class of citizens, to the higher circles of society, and to the orthodox church. And would not the testimony of such a man be received as first-class evidence in any court?

Be all this as it may, however, the human spirit Abraham, to whom the prayer in question was offered, and whose testimony cannot be disputed, certainly heard that prayer and replied to it. In doing this Abraham not only established the fact that human spirits can and do hear and answer prayers, but also the fact that it is perfectly right and proper for them to do so. Those of you act wisely, then, who call upon their spirit friends, who invoke the aid of the saints and the angels in heaven. And you who neglect to do this will some day, when it is forever too late, regret your folly in failing to secure the assistance of some one who has a little more influence at heaven's headquarters than you have yourselves.

It is true that in the case before us Abraham did not grant the relief prayed for by his petitioner. His refusal to do so, however, was based, not on the ground that himself was not a proper person to hear and to answer prayers, but simply on the ground that this damned man was not a proper person to receive the relief for which he prayed.

When implored to send Lazarus to earth to warn this unhappy man's brethren, Abraham again refused on other grounds, but did not so much as intimate that he had no power to grant such prayers, nor that human spirits like Lazarus were unable to return to earth, and to communicate with men. Had it been either impossible or improper for him to send spirits to communicate with men, he would doubtless have mentioned this fact as the best of all reasons for not granting the petitioner's prayer. Instead of assigning any such reasons, however, he speaks of the sending of Lazarus to earth as of something which he could do, and which, on a proper occasion, he would do.

Besides all this, Jesus, who tells the story, certainly means to represent this damned man as proceeding in the only proper manner to obtain that which he desired. He was using this man's case to illustrate the utterly hopeless condition of the inmates of hell, and in order to make that condition appear thus utterly hopeless he had to represent this man as appealing in a proper manner to the proper authority, and as having his petition rejected by that authority. To have represented him as making a mistake in praying to Abraham would not have been to represent his case as hopeless at all; since, by correcting that mistake, and appealing to the proper authority, he might still have obtained that for which he prayed. Before any case can be pronounced utterly hopeless it must be properly presented to the highest tribunal before which such cases can come, and must be properly tried and lost before that tribunal. If, then, the case of this damned man was utterly hopeless, as Jesus certainly means to teach that it was, then in this case we have positive proof, not only that Abraham was the proper authority to try the case, but also that there was no appeal from his decision. In this case, then, we have conclusive evidence, from the highest possible source, that some human spirits of a higher grade, like Abraham, are placed in high authority in heaven, and that they grant or reject petitions, send messages to earth by other spirits, etc. We also have equally conclusive evidence, from the same high source, that other spirits of a lower grade, like Lazarus, are placed under the authority of superior spirits, and that they have inferior duties assigned them, such as bearing messages to men, etc. While thus employed bearing messages, etc., these spirits would be angels, and in the Bible would, of course, be so called. It was doubtless by a band of such angels that Lazarus was borne to Abraham's bosom.

God is undeniably the source of all power, and of all judgment; and yet he does not in person exercise this all-power, and this all-judgment. In Matt. xxviii, 18, we read: "And Jesus came and spake unto them, saying, All power is given unto me in heaven and in earth." In John v, 22, as I have already quoted, we also read: "For the father judgeth no man, but hath committed all judgment unto the son." This all-power, this all-judgment, thus delegated to Jesus, included, of course, the power to re-delegate a portion, or even all, of this same power and this same judgment to certain other parties whom he might see fit to make his agents or representatives; and this re-delegation of power and of judgment he proceeded at once to make. As soon as he had declared that all power was given to him "in heaven and in earth," he added: "Go ye, therefore, and teach all nations, baptizing them in the name of the Father, and of the Son, and of the Holy Ghost: teaching them to observe all things whatsoever I have commanded you : and, lo, I am with you alway, even unto the end of the world."

In these his final instructions Jesus refers to all the commands which he had ever given to his apostles, and requires them to teach all nations to observe them all. Mark has him on this same occasion repeat some of the former commands to which he refers, and which were to heal the sick, to speak with new tongues, to cast out devils, to raise the dead, and, in short, to do all the works which himself had been wont to do, and even "greater works than these." He also promises to be with them in these works, "alway, even unto the end of the world."

These things prove beyond all contradiction that Jesus did not address the apostles in their individual capacities. Of course, he could not have expected them, as individuals, to continue on earth, engaged in these works, "alway, even unto the end of the world." He could have addressed such language to them only in their official or representative capacities. In this case he would, of course, include all their successors in office, and all others of whom the apostles stood as the representatives.

Whatever commands, then, whatever powers, and whatever promises were given to the apostles, were through them given to "them that believe," of all nations, and of all ages. If, then, Jesus was not an impostor, all those commands are still binding upon his followers, all those powers still possessed, and all those works still performed by them. If you deny all this, you simply make Jesus a liar, and overturn the Christian religion. If you admit it all, you admit the truth and the heavenly character of Spiritualism. You admit, too, that the Spiritualists, whom these signs follow, are of "them that believe," and of "them who shall be heirs of salvation." In either case you reduce, as usual, to mere pretenders—to those who are to be damned.

You charge me with advocating a doctrine of the Catholic church. I admit the charge, and am glad that, in the Catholic church, I have so respectable an ally. I do not advocate anything, however, because it is a doctrine of that or of any church. I advocate nothing but truth, and that I advocate simply because it is truth. If the Catholics happen to be in possession of a truth of which you are destitute, so much the better for them, and so much the worse for you. I am not bound to reject a truth because they teach it, nor because you fail to teach it. If you would rather go to hell on a lie taught by your own church than to heaven on a truth taught by Catholics and Spiritualists, all right. Go your way. I have not the slightest objection. It is your privilege, and then there are not half so many go to hell as ought to go. I am not like most other ministers of the gospel, trying to rob the devil of his just dues. Besides this, you will find hell full of just such men as yourselves—men who loved creeds more than they loved truth. With these persons you will be able to form more congenial associations than you could form anywhere else. All I have to say to you then, is—go to hell!

While Jesus was on earth, acting in his human capacity, and as one under the authority of another, he dealt with men in person, just as a man deals with his fellow-men. When, however, his mortal part put on immortality, when he resumed his divine character, he ceased to deal with men in person, and began to deal with them exclusively through agents or representatives. Since his ascension into heaven he has not, so far as we know, performed in person a single act relating to men. As we have already seen, he has given to his agents on earth full power to do all those things which he was accustomed to do himself when he was upon earth, and all that he would now do himself if he were upon earth to-day. To his agents in heaven he has also given equally ample powers. He has made them kings and judges, and put them to work helping carry on his universal government. To every one, however humble, he has given something to do.

In 1 Cor. vi, 2, 3, we read: "Do ye not know that the saints shall judge the world? And if the world shall be judged by you, are ye unworthy to judge the smallest matters? Know ye not that we shall judge angels? How much more things that pertain to this life?" In all the cases mentioned here the act of judging is spoken of in exactly the same sense. From this it is evident that the judging of angels and others in heaven is just as real as is the judging of "things that pertain to this life." The saints in heaven, then, are real, not figurative, judges.

In Luke ix, 49, 50, we read: "And John answered

and said, Master, we saw one casting out devils in thy name, and we forbade him, because he followeth not with us. And Jesus said unto him, Forbid him not: for he that is not against us is for us." From this we learn that those who do the works of Jesus are approved of him, and are not to be forbidden, though they do not follow with his visible church. This is peculiarly applicable to that large and respectable class of Spiritualists who, like myself, outside of all church organizations, are faithfully laboring in the cause of truth and humanity.

On the exclusive testimony of the Bible and of the Christian church I have now fully proved, not only that spiritual communications between men and spirits do take place, but also that a regular system of such communications is absolutely necessary to the fulfilling of the commands of Jesus, and to the conducting of God's general government. I will now briefly recapitulate my arguments, and then close.

1. I have proved that "there is joy in the presence of the angels of God over one sinner that repenteth." This renders constant communications between earth and heaven absolutely necessary. Without such communications the inhabitants of heaven would not know when to rejoice, nor over what sinner to rejoice.

2. I have proved that there are certain spirits in heaven, called elders, who minister before the throne of Jesus, and who present to him "the prayers of the saints." In proving this I have proved that Jesus does not hear the prayers of the saints directly, but receives them through the hands of the elders who minister around his throne. In order that they may themselves receive the prayers which they are

to present to Jesus, it is absolutely necessary that these elders be in constant communication with those who are praying on earth.

3. By the case of Lazarus I have proved that when they die they are borne to their places of future abode by spirits who, because acting as messengers, are called angels. This, again, renders constant communications between the spirit world and our own absolutely necessary. Without such communications the spirit angels would not know just when and where to go after each new-born spirit on earth. From this case I also prove that, at the time of a death, if at no other time, there are spirits among us. At such a time there must of necessity be present, for a moment, at least, the spirit of the one who has just died, and the spirits that have come to bear him to his future home.

4. I have proved that whatsoever the apostles should bind or loose upon earth was to be bound or loosed in heaven. This, again, renders absolutely necessary a constant intercourse between the inhabitants of earth and those of heaven. Without such intercourse those who are to do the binding and the loosing in heaven would not know when a thing has been bound or loosed on earth, nor what that thing might be.

5. I have proved that the followers of Jesus were to speak with new tongues, or in languages unknown to themselves. In order that they may be able to do this it is absolutely necessary for some spirit that understands the unknown language to take possession of their organs of speech, and through them communicate whatever may be necessary in that

unknown language. Persons whose organs of speech are thus taken possession of and used by spirits become what we now call speaking mediums. Of these we have thousands to-day.

6. I have proved that Jesus, acting in his human capacity, called up spirits and conversed with them, thus demonstrating both the practicability and the propriety of doing these things. I have also proved that he commanded and empowered his followers to do these same things. Persons who thus see spirits and converse with them are what we now call clairvoyant and clairaudient mediums. Of these we have many thousands to-day.

7. I have proved that during all time, "even unto the end of the world," the followers of Jesus were to cast out evil spirits. In order that they may be able to do this it is absolutely necessary that such spirits actually have possession of certain persons, and that those who are to cast them out have power to discern their presence, and to communicate to them the order to depart. All these things render Spiritualism an absolute necessity. These works are as truly performed at the present time as they ever were.

8. I have proved that "alway, even unto the end of the world," the followers of Jesus were to "raise the dead," that is, to call back the spirits of the dead for any proper purpose whatever, whether that purpose be to have them reinhabit their forsaken tenements of clay, or merely to have them commune with us on other matters. All this, again, renders Spiritualism an absolute necessity, as well as an imperative duty.

9. I have proved that if you have our spirit friends

of choice cease to commune with us, you make them worse than the damned; that if you have them cease through compulsion, you make God worse than the devil, and that if you do not have them cease at all, you have Spiritualism in its full and glorious operation.

LECTURE IV.

SPIRITUAL MEDIUMSHIP.

Having in my three preceding lectures professedly acted simply as an attorney for Spiritualism, having accepted as truth—whether I believed it to be so or not—whatever testimony my opponents adduced in favor of Spiritualism through their own witnesses, the Bible and the Christian church, a question might arise in some of your minds as to whether I am or am not myself a believer in Spiritualism. To this question I reply that I am now a believer in this beautiful philosophy. I am only a recent convert, however, and my conversion was not effected by any of the Biblical and the church testimony given in the preceding lectures. It was effected by means of overwhelming tests that compelled me to believe. A description of these tests I shall not give in this course of lectures. Were I to describe them, they would be no tests to you. They would be hearsay evidence, and this you do not want unless you get it from the Bible or the church. You want direct tests—tests addressed to your own senses. These you can obtain from any good test-medium. Should you, in seeking these tests, find a fraud among the mediums, you need not be either surprised or discouraged. I found many such frauds, and I expect still to find many more. Though you admit that there have been many false Christs, you still believe that there is one true Christ. Apply this same principle then to the mediums, and you will not err. A belief in Spiritualism renders me a better and a happier man; and I have no doubt that it would have the same effect upon yourselves.

Having, in preceding lectures, fully established the truth of all the claims of Spiritualism, I propose now to consider the philosophy or the *modus operandi* of Spiritual Mediumship. I do not hold that there is anything supernatural in what are known as Spiritual Manifestations. To me they appear to be just as strictly in accordance with the laws of nature as are any of the other phenomena with which we are acquainted. Indeed, I do not know any such thing as the supernatural. Supply the necessary conditions, and communications between a man and a spirit become just as easy and just as natural as are those between one man and another. The presence of these necessary conditions constitutes what is called Spiritual Mediumship.

On account of their infrequency, certain phenomena strike us as very wonderful; and when we are ignorant of their true causes, we are easily led to believe that those causes are supernatural. In former times the occurrence of eclipses, the appearance of comets, etc., were almost universally regarded with superstitious dread, as supernatural phenomena indicating the wrath of the gods, and portending some dire calamity to the inhabitants of the earth.

The extremely ignorant still regard these phenomena in very nearly the same light. In all cases, however, the true causes of all these phenomena, when ascertained, have proved to be just as natural as are the causes of the most common phenomena with which we are acquainted. We never need a god to account for any phenomena of which we know the real causes. All gods stand as the representatives of causes which we do not understand. The more ignorant men are, therefore, the more they need gods, and the more firmly they believe in the existence of such beings. Infidelity, or unbelief in the existence of the gods, never prevails except among the educated and the intelligent. It is a fact too well known to require any proof that in all countries the most ignorant classes are the most zealous religionists, no matter what the religion may be. Enlighten the people, and you ruin the trade of the priests. Educated and intelligent men rarely, if ever, become zealous worshipers of any god, unless they see money, fame popularity, or something else equally real and equally earthly in the enterprise.

For my own part, I need no gods, and consequently I have no belief in their existence. Like space, Nature is everywhere present, and a thing can no more be outside of Nature than it can be outside of space. This is true of all things, from the formation of a dew-drop to that of the entire universe. All motions and all formations are equally the results of properties and forces eternally inherent in matter. None of them are produced by the interposition of divine power.

As we have traveled over but a small portion of space, so we have become acquainted with but a small portion of Nature and of her powers. To limit these powers then to the few phenomena with which we are acquainted, and to assume that all those phenomena are supernatural, whose causes lie beyond these limits, is just as absurd as it would be to limit the extent of space in like manner to the small portion which we have visited, and then to assume that all those objects are superspacial which lie beyond the narrow limits thus assigned. And yet men have committed this very absurdity. They have assigned limits to Nature, and then placed certain phenomena beyond those limits. As the result of this absurdity, they had to assume something in the place of nature to account for those phenomena which, as they erroneously thought, lay beyond the limits of nature. This assumption gave rise to all those imaginary beings called gods. Were we to absurdly assign limits to space, then of necessity we would be compelled to assume something, in lieu of space, to contain those objects which, in our erroneous opinions, would lie beyond the limits of space. Whatever we might call the thing thus assumed, it would be just as real as are any of the gods whose existence is a mere assumption, rendered necessary, as we have seen, by a precisely similar absurdity.

Some men assumed only one god, and ascribed to him a diversity of powers sufficient to account for all those phenomena whose real causes were unknown. By far the greater number, however, assumed many gods, to each of whom they ascribed the production of a particular class of phenomena. Whether many or few, these gods were all equally the creatures of men's imaginations, and all equally had their origin in dark ages, and among ignorant and superstitious men. No god ever did, or ever could, take his rise in an enlightened age and among an intelligent people.

All the gods, too, are equally useless. The phenomena which they are assumed to produce, having their real causes in nature, would be produced just the same without these assumed causes as with them. We might assume something, in lieu of space, to contain all those objects which lie beyond certain limits; and yet, notwithstanding our assumption, those objects would continue to lie in space just the same. The thing assumed, being entirely imaginary, would evidently be entirely useless. So of the equally imaginary gods. Neither nature nor space can possibly be absent from any place, and hence nothing can possibly be beyond either of them. In a former work, entitled, "Deity Analyzed," I more fully considered these things, and more fully proved the truth of all that I now assert concerning them. I merely glance at them now in order that you may understand why it is that, in considering the various phases of mediumship, I leave all of the gods entirely out of the question, and appeal to nature alone. I shall no longer act as a mere attorney of Spiritualism, and shall no longer accept as true any testimony which I do not believe to be true. I shall fearlessly attack the testimony of the Bible, of the church, or of any other party, if I believe that testimony to be false; and I shall fearlessly hold up for ridicule anything that I regard as ridiculous.

In treating this subject, I shall have to take it for granted that you are all believers in what is usually termed "the immortality of the soul," and that consequently you are all believers also in the existence of that class of beings called spirits. For those who do not believe in these things, I can on the present occasion do but little. They need tests, and these I am not prepared to give. These will be given by any good test medium.

Taking it for granted, then, that spirits do exist, it follows of necessity that they must exist somewhere; and since, as we have already seen, nature, like space, exists everywhere; it also follows of equal necessity that they must exist within the domain of nature just as we do, and subject to her laws just as we are. In preceding lectures I fully proved, by testimony which no believer in the Christian religion will dare to reject, that spirits do exist, and do communicate with men. Taking these facts for granted, therefore, I shall proceed at once to the consideration of the means by which the communications in question are rendered practicable.

Spiritual communications of all kinds may be reduced to the following five distinct classes—viz.: 1. Those made by raps, and by other physical signs; 2. Those made by writing, through the hand of a medium; 3. Those made by speaking, through the lips of a medium; 4. Those made by clairvoyance and clairaudience; 5. Those made by inspiration. These five methods of communication involve five different phases of mediumship, which I will now proceed to explain.

The most common method by which spirits communicate with men is by means of raps, or physical signals of some kind. This is a species of natural language, and is usually the only method by which spirits can communicate with men. Indeed, even this method is practicable only under certain conditions, which I will explain.

Two living men may be so situated relatively to each other that in order to carry on any correspondence with each other they would be compelled to resort to this very method. Let A be a man who can hear and speak, but who is totally blind; let B be another man who can see and hear, but who has no voice at all. Now, let B pay a visit to A. Since B cannot speak, and since A cannot see him approach, B, you perceive, is compelled to rap, or to make some other physical signal, addressed to A's sense of hearing, in order that his presence may be made known to A. Let us suppose, then, that B raps. "Who is there?" asks B. No answer. And why not? Because, as you already know, B cannot speak, and because no number of raps would indicate his name. "Did not some one rap?" asks A. Three raps answer, "Yes." "Who is it, then?" No response. "Can you not speak?" Two raps answer, "No." You now perceive that B can do nothing except answer "Yes" or "No" to direct questions. A, however, fails to ask such questions as would enable B to thus make known the object of his visit. A then asks: "Could you spell out the object of your visit by rapping at the proper letters, if I were to slowly repeat the alphabet?" Three raps answer, "Yes." A now proceeds to repeat the alphabet aloud, and whenever he reaches the proper letter of a word, one rap is heard. Thus slowly, but surely, A learns the object of B's visit. And now, let me ask, could A, without the aid of a third party, have gained this information in any other way? Suppose we blindfold some man in the audience, and then let one of you from the opposite side of the hall, without using your voice, undertake to communicate to him some particular message, how would you do this, except by raps, or by some similar physical signals?

In these supposed cases we have placed the parties communicating in precisely the same situation, relatively to each other, as that in which a man and a spirit are placed when undertaking to carry out with each other a similar correspondence. Men whose spiritual eyes are not opened are totally blind to all spiritual objects, while spirits are totally voiceless to men whose spiritual ears are not opened. The consciousness of such men can be reached only through their physical senses. Hence the necessity, in communicating directly with such men, of the raps, or other physical effects, produced by the spirits upon tables or other material objects. By agreement between the parties communicating, certain forms, numbers, and combinations of these raps, motions, etc., are fixed upon as definite signs, by means of which communications are made. This method of communicating with spirits was known and used among the Romans and the early Christians. And now, having shown that it is a natural and necessary method, and not at all trivial, I will proceed to explain the means by which spirits are enabled to produce the raps and other physical phenomena involved in this method.

Most of you are doubtless aware that all men possess certain magnetic powers which constitute them weak magnets. Many of you, however, may not be aware that these magnetic powers inhere principally in the spirits of men, and not in their bodies, and yet such has been found to be undeniably the fact.

After the departure of the spirit, the body of a man possesses very little, if any, of this power. The power, then, evidently accompanies the spirit. Indeed, it is now known that all volition, all thought, all sensation, and all consciousness depend upon the power of magnetism. In order to have any conscious existence at all, then, spirits must of necessity possess magnetism.

Though all men are really positive in their magnetic conditions, some of them are negative as compared with others. This fact accounts for the well-known attractions and repulsions that exist among men, and especially between persons of opposite sex. By a well-known law of magnetism, two persons who are alike in their magnetic conditions will repel, while two others, who are unlike in this respect, will attract each other. If those who repel each other be thrown much together, a strong dislike, amounting sometimes to intense hatred, is apt to spring up between them. Between those who attract each other, a strong friendship is apt to spring up. Indeed, other conditions being all right, a man very positive in his magnetic condition, and a woman very negative in hers, when thrown much together, will inevitably fall deeply in love with each other. They become restless and unhappy when deprived of each other's society. When they press each other's hands—and this they are sure to do—a thrill of pleasure pervades their whole beings, and when their lips happen to meet—as they sometimes do—their bliss becomes absolutely indescribable.

In this latter case, the unlike magnetisms of the two parties are striving to flow together, and to thus establish an equilibrium. And it is now a well-known fact that these unlike magnetisms do flow together even through considerable distances, and through intervening obstacles. If the current of magnetism flowing between two such persons be made to pass through a liquid which holds certain substances in solution, a very obvious chemical action may be made to take place among the substances thus held in solution. This proves the power of the magnetic current. This same power, however, is often proved in another way. If the one you most dearly love be in great danger, or great trouble, you generally have an intuition of the fact, more or less vivid, even though you be many miles away.

If between two persons, such as I have been describing, a metallic substance be made to intervene, the magnetic currents will pass through it so freely that no raps or other sensible effects are likely to be produced. If the intervening substance be glass, the magnetic currents will not pass at all; and hence, in this case, as in the other, no sensible effects are likely to be produced. If, however, the intervening substance be wood, the magnetic currents will pass through it; but, being partially obstructed in their passage, they will be likely to produce certain percussive sounds which we call raps. These sounds proceed from an exceedingly feeble action of a certain form of that mighty force which sometimes in an instant shivers the giant oak into a thousand fragments, and shakes the solid earth with its terrific thunderings.

In order to produce raps, table-tippings, etc., by means of human magnetism, a circular table, well-joined, and free from varnish, should be provided. Around this table a circle of from six to twelve persons should be formed. In this circle the two sexes should be equally represented. In their magnetic conditions the men should be as unlike the women as possible, and they should be seated alternately—that is, first a man, then a woman, then a man, and so on. To some extent the magnetic conditions of persons may be determined by their temperaments. An efficient circle may usually be formed of a certain number of men with black hair, black eyes, and dark complexion, and an equal number of women with light hair, blue eyes, and fair complexion. Perfect harmony must prevail among the members of the circle. All should be willing to give the experiment a fair trial. Anyone may prevent success by destroying the conditions upon which success depends.

Having in this manner formed the circle, let the members join hands upon the table, and then fix their thoughts intently upon its center, and listen for the raps which they desire to hear there. Such a circle is not likely to sit long without raps. If a good medium be present, raps will be heard almost immediately.

When the raps have become so fully established that questions are answered promptly, then let the unbroken circle of hands be raised an inch or more from the table, and moved backward and forward over the table, about as fast as the table would oscillate if once set in motion. If the legs of the table be close together, as they should be for this experiment, the table will soon begin to oscillate in unison with the circle of hands. Let these oscillations be noticed, and as they increase, let the movement of the circle of hands be gradually changed from a horizontal to a kind of rocking motion, so as to favor these oscillations. Let these movements be continued until the table tips beyond its centre of gravity, and falls upon the floor.

If you can ever start the table to moving at all, you can always overturn it, since the moment it begins to oscillate both gravity and inertia come to your aid, and enable you to increase that motion. The currents of magnetism which pass from the circle of hands to the table may be compared to an infinite number of highly elastic but invisible threads which pull the table in whatever direction the circle of hands is being moved.

I am now prepared to hear it objected that I have disproved the truth of this phase of Spiritualism by showing that genuine raps, table-tippings, etc., may be produced, without the aid of spirits, by human magnetism alone. Very well. I fully understand the difficulty into which I seem to have fallen, and I have purposely encountered it. If the difficulty exist only in appearance, I will remove it; if it exist in reality, then let this phase of mediumship be condemned. If, in all its phases, Spiritualism cannot bear the tests of reason, of science, and of common sense, then it ought to go down, just as all religions, founded on the idea of a personal god, are bound to go, whenever they are subjected to these same tests.

My explanation, however, does not at all tend to disprove the truth of this phase of Spiritualism. It merely shows how careful we ought to be in our investigations, lest we indiscriminately ascribe to spiritual agency phenomena, some of which may perchance be produced by the agency of men; and lest, on the other hand, we, in like manner, ascribe to human agency phenomena, some of which, perchance, may be produced by the agency of spirits.

As the fact that swans can fly is no proof at all that eagles cannot do the same, so the fact that men can produce certain phenomena is no proof at all that spirits cannot produce the same. Your objection, then, is entirely without foundation. Indeed, my explanation is a strong argument in favor of the truth of Spiritualism. Men are simply spirits encased in coverings of flesh, and spirits are simply men minus these fleshly coverings. Unless, then, you can prove that the phenomena in question are produced by the fleshly coverings of the spirits that surround the table, you are bound to admit that they are produced by the spirits themselves. Such proof, however, you can never give. The dead bodies of men are found to possess none of the magnetic power upon which these phenomena depend. Not even one rap can be produced by the dead bodies of a dozen mediums. Not so, however, with disembodied spirits. To say nothing of the thousands of careful tests made yearly by many of the most honest and intelligent men of the present time, all history, both sacred and profane, is filled with accounts of the achievements of disembodied spirits. The opposers of Spiritualism may, and actually do, produce genuine raps, table tippings, etc., but when they pretend that, by so doing, they disprove the truth of Spiritualism, they simply expose either their own gross ignorance, or their own lamentable want of common honesty. Let them leave their own spirits and all other spirits entirely out of the experiment—let them surround the table with their fleshly bodies alone; and then, and not till then, can they justly claim that, by the production of the phenomena in question, they have succeeded in casting even a doubt upon the truth of Spiritualism. Even this test would amount to no proof damaging to Spiritualism, for although fleshly bodies might produce these phenomena, spirits might still produce the same.

For the sake of the argument, however, let us, for a moment, admit that, in proving the power of men to produce certain phenomena, you have proved the inability of spirits to produce the same. In other words, let us admit, as proved by you, that there is no power common to both men and spirits. Then, indeed, according to your wish, we prove that because men can produce raps, table tippings, etc., spirits cannot produce any of these phenomena. But we do not stop here. We also prove that because men can see, hear, speak, move, taste, smell, feel, think, etc., spirits can not do any of these things. In other words, as you plainly see, we prove spirits entirely out of conscious existence. So much, then, for this vaunted proof of the self-styled exposers of Spiritualism. They prove either too much or too little.

Since the second and the third phases of mediumship, writing and speaking under spirit control, both depend upon precisely the same principles, I will treat them together. Like the first phase, these two phases depend, for their operation, upon the power of magnetism.

Although our knowledge of magnetism is confined entirely in its effects, yet we are as sure of its existence as we are of that of heat, of light, of air, or of anything else. With many of the laws of magnetism we are also acquainted. We know that its power decreases inversely as the square of the distance from the magnet or body which contains it. We know, too, that one magnet will suspend, invert, or in some other way control the action of another magnet of less power than its own. For illustration, let us take a small magnet whose power, within a certain sphere of which itself is the center, we will say is one. Let this magnet be placed in contact with another magnet whose power is five. It is evident that the entire sphere pervaded by the power of the smaller magnet is now pervaded also by the five-fold greater power of the larger magnet. It is also evident that whatever objects lie within the sphere of the smaller magnet, and which, were no greater power present, would obey the power of that magnet, must now disregard this weaker power, and obey the much greater power of the larger magnet. By a greater power than its own, the smaller magnet is mesmerized, so to speak, or thrown into a magnetic sleep. For the time it has lost its individuality, and has become, as it were, a part of the larger magnet.

Now, let us suppose that these two magnets are two persons, of whom A is the weaker and B the stronger. On being brought together, A is immediately mesmerized or thrown into a magnetic sleep by the greater power of B. For the time, A's individuality is lost, and his hands, his organs of speech, etc., being now under the influence of a stronger power than his own, are bound to obey that stronger power, and to write, to speak, etc., as ordered by that controlling power. That one person can sometimes thus bring another under his control is now a well-established fact. I therefore offer no proofs.

Thus far we have regarded both A and B as living persons. Let us now, however, take B's body from him, and let him, as a spirit, with his powerful magnetism undiminished, again pervade A's magnetic sphere. Again brought under his control, A again writes and speaks according to his will. A is now a writing and speaking medium, such as have existed in all ages of the world.

Having fully explained the three lower phases of mediumship, in which the medium is a mere instrument, I will now proceed to the consideration of those higher phases, clairvoyance, clairaudience, and inspiration, in which the medium becomes the companion and the equal of spirits.

If spirits exist at all, as sentient and intelligent beings, it is evident that they must of necessity possess all the senses and faculties, such as sight, hearing, feeling, thinking, etc., which are necessary to constitute them such beings. To make them blind, deaf, dumb, motionless, and devoid of thought and of feeling, would be simply to deny their existence. Since, then, we have taken it for granted that they do exist, we are bound also to take it for granted that they do possess sight, hearing, and all the other senses and faculties essential to such existence. All this being taken for granted, it is evident that if the spirit itself exists before the death of the body it must exist with all the essential senses and faculties of such existence. To have all these senses and faculties created after death, would leave nothing to go forth out of the body at the time of death. Such a creation, therefore, would not be a continuation of man's existence at all. It would be simply the annihilation of man, and the creation of an entirely new race of beings.

From this it is evident that in the present life all men are dualistic beings, having one full set of physical organs, physical senses, etc., adapted to bring them into relation with the material world; and another set of spiritual organs, spiritual senses, etc., adapted to bring them into relation with the spiritual world. St. Paul very clearly teaches this truth in his outer man and his inner man, in his natural body and his spiritual body. Indeed, no one who believes in the immortality of the soul can deny this truth. It is true, however, that having to deal mostly with the material world, our spiritual faculties in the present life are rarely called into action. The consequence is that for want of use during the present state of existence our spirital faculties are usually allowed to lie in a dormant or undeveloped condition. Indeed, like the rudimentary wings of the butterfly in its chrysalis state this undeveloped or rudimentary condition of our spiritual faculties during the present life is undoubtedly their normal condition, and should be allowed to continue until Nature, in her own time and manner, brings about a development. The forced development of our spiritual faculties during the present life is as unnatural as would be the forced development of the wings of a butterfly in its chrysalis state. This forced and unnatural development then, whether it be produced by spiritual developing circles, or by religious revival meetings, should be emphatically discouraged. What we want in this material world is physical development. We want bodies which are the perfection of physical health, strength, and beauty. From such bodies, and from such alone, will Nature, in her own good time, bring forth forms which shall be the perfection of spiritual health, strength, and beauty. From a chrysalis, which is rotting with disease, and which changes before the natural time, Nature cannot produce a butterfly perfect in health, strength, and beauty. So from a man who is a bundle of diseases and deformities, and who changes before the natural time, Nature cannot produce a spirit perfect in health, strength, and beauty.

If our ministers of the gospel would properly consider this matter, and would turn their attention to the production of perfectly developed, strong, healthy, and beautiful bodies for the people, then their labors would result in real good. To people thus physically perfect, this life would be a real blessing; this world a land of flowers, of sunlight, and of joy. In their great eagerness, however, to gain converts and dollars, our ministers of the gospel, as a class, are now doing positive harm. They are turning away the attention of the people from a real good that might be attained, and directing it to an imaginary good that can not be attained. To a great extent their congregations are made up of persons whose first births have been sadly mismanaged, whose physical conditions have been extremely unfavorable, and whose bodies in consequence are so badly put together, so shaky, so full of aches and of pains, that were they not held together by artificial means they would be liable at any moment to fall to pieces. To the unhappy dwellers in these wretched tenements this life is not a blessing, this world is not a land of flowers, of sunlight, and of joy. To them it is just what in their unutterably sad wailings they represent it to be—"a vale of tears, a wilderness of woe." And yet because it is unpopular to do so, and because it does not pay, our ministers of the gospel make no effort to remove the causes of all this misery. They make no effort to secure perfect first births, perfect physical conditions, to future generations. Because it is popular to do so, and because it pays, they constantly harp upon the second birth, and the blissful conditions of the spirit world. This is wrong. These ministers ought to know and ought to teach that from the moment of conception, and even before, to the utmost limit of spirit-life, man is under the control of Nature's laws. They ought to know and ought to teach that any violation of these laws is inevitably attended with suffering. They ought to know and ought to teach that Nature has divided human existence into three grand periods: The present life; the antenatal life which precedes the present; and the spiritual life which follows it; that each succeeding period is an almost infinite advance upon the preceding, but that any untimely passage from a lower to a higher period is a great if not an irreparable misfortune; that to undergo the second birth—the change called death, the birth from this life into the life of spirits, before the natural time—seventy years or more—is just as much an abortion, and just as much a misfortune to the subject of it, as is a similarly untimely birth into this life.

I do not wish to bring a pang into the hearts of those parents who have been wont to solace their grief for the loss of their children with the thought that by an untimely, and consequently an unnatural death, those children have been rendered better off. I wish I could truthfully say that I believe such to be the fact. As a conscientious man, however, I must say that until all its uses are attained—until as fully ripe fruit we pass from it—this life is by far the best life there is for us. Those suffer a great disadvantage who make an abortive or untimely entrance into spirit-life. Were this not true—were it a fact that by death children are rendered better off—then, since it is always our duty to better the condition of our children, it would undeniably be our duty to hurry them out of this life into a better one. Comforting as is the doctrine, however, that untimely death renders our children better off, few sane persons really believe it. Insane persons have really believed it, and have actually slain their children to render them better off. From all these things it is evident that in this life our principal concern should be the first birth, the perfect development of the body, the physical conditions generally. I have made this rather lengthy digression because of the evil that is being done, not only by the teachings of ministers of the gospel, but also by those of many Spiritualistic leaders, who, with wasted bodies all trembling from nervous prostration and agony, are running wild after spiritual power and spiritual development, which they do not yet need, and totally neglecting to seek the physical power and the physical development which they do so greatly need. Give me the perfectly developed bodies—all health, strength, and beauty—to which suffering is unknown, and I will guarantee that Nature, in her own good time and manner, will make the spirits all right. If you can only get a good first birth, you need not trouble yourself about the second birth. That will be all right.

When, however, the uses of this state of existence have all been accomplished, when the weights of life have run down, and its pendulum has ceased to vibrate; when nature's own full time has come for this mortal to put on immortality, then the spiritual faculties come as naturally into action as do the lungs upon our first entrance into the present life. Sometimes, also, without actually suffering death, a man may enter into an abnormal condition, called trance, which so nearly resembles death that, for the time, his physical faculties are almost as fully suspended as they would be in death itself. While in this condition the same necessities which death produces are upon him, and, of course, the same immediate results follow. His spiritual faculties are aroused to action, and he sees spirits and converses with them just as spirits see and converse with one another. He is now, indeed, in the spirit-world, but only as a transient visitor. He must soon return to his physical condition. The power to thus see spirits, and to hear them speak, constitutes what we call clairvoyance and clairaudience. Some persons have power to enter into this trance condition, and to become clairvoyant and clairaudient at pleasure. A few use their spiritual faculties without going into any trance at all. These latter persons, simultaneously using both their physical and their spiritual faculties, are, of course, at the same time, in direct communication with both worlds. This condition is a very desirable one, provided it come naturally, and without injury to the physical powers. It should never be attained, however, by any forcing process.

Clairvoyance and clairaudience may generally be induced by fasting until the body becomes extremely attenuated and the physical powers almost exhausted. This is especially the case, if, while fasting, the thoughts be kept fixed upon heavenly or spiritual things. Under the erroneous idea that it is a virtue to do so, the devotees of all religions, and of all ages, have been accustomed to induce this state by subjecting themselves to long-continued fastings, prayers, and meditations. By thus all using the same means they have all, naturally enough, attained the same end, no matter what religions they have professed, nor what gods they have worshiped. When greatly emaciated by long illness, most persons, just before death, are apt to become clairvoyant and clairaudient. They then behold the angelic forms and hear the heavenly music of their spirit friends, who are waiting to welcome them to their bright abodes amid the fadeless beauties of the summer-land.

Under certain conditions clairvoyance and clairaudience may also be induced by human magnetism. Sometimes the magnetism is supplied by the "laying on of hands," or other manipulations of a special operator. When this operator is a priest, or a body of priests, and the subject is a candidate for holy orders, the operation is called imparting the holy ghost. It must be confessed, however, that this formal laying on of hands, under the pretense of imparting the holy ghost, very rarely produces clairvoyance or any other sensible effect.

The magnetism is more frequently supplied by a large number of persons, of both sexes, crowded together as closely as possible, and all highly wrought up on some subject, as is the case in what are called revival meetings. Surrounding such a crowd of persons, especially in an ill-ventilated room, there is a powerful magnetic sphere, near the center of which, if very susceptible persons be placed, they will become magnetized, and will finally, if the operation be continued, experience that peculiar sensation which is usually denominated "getting religion," or "conversion." When fully magnetized, such persons feel a "joy unspeakable and full of glory," and sometimes, becoming clairvoyant and clairaudient, they see "heaven opened," as they express it, and behold things of indescribable beauty, and hear music of unutterable sweetness.

In order to expedite the work of conversion, the candidates should be kept in the center of the greatest excitement, and the crowd around them should be packed as closely as possible. If practicable, this crowd should be composed entirely of believers. The presence of an infidel will tend to retard, if not to prevent, the success of the experiment. It is very difficult for a man to become converted in the back part of the church, on the outside of the crowd of people. This is especially the case if there be unbelievers and scoffers about him, and if he be near an open door or window, where the fresh air drives away the moist, magnetic atmosphere of the room, on which his conversion principally depends.

During the progress of this experiment the leader of the meeting, or some other good magnetizer, should, as often as convenient, approach the candidates, clasp their hands, place his hands upon their heads, gently slap their backs, etc. In this way the advantages of special manipulation may be added to those of a dense and magnetic crowd. All good revivalists understand these things, and act accordingly. As to the bodily position of the candidates, I would recommend the old, Methodistic plan, which I have myself practiced with great success, of having them all kneel together at what is called a mourner's bench, or anxious seat. By this position we prevent their attention from being called off by what is going on around them, and thus we secure the conditions most favorable for their conversion.

Besides all these things, the candidates, if possible, should be induced to observe a strict fast, from the moment they engage in the experiment, till their conversion is completed. By the pernicious habit of allowing them to eat heartily, during the recesses of the meetings, their conversion is always greatly retarded, and frequently entirely prevented. In Acts x, 9–11, we read: "Peter went up upon the housetop to pray, about the sixth hour: and he became very hungry, and would have eaten, but while they made ready he fell into a trance, and saw heaven opened," etc. Peter had doubtless been fasting a long time. At any rate, "he became very hungry," just the right condition in which to become entranced, and to see "heaven opened." Had Peter not been fasting, it is not at all likely that he would have been thus entranced. To secure such entrancement it is generally necessary, by means of fasting or other methods of depletion, to so reduce the physical powers that they almost cease to act. In this way the fleshly covering of the spirit is made to hang as it were, so loosely, that the spirit attains almost the same degree of freedom that it would attain by the full dissolution of the body. To some extent this same physical condition of attenuation is also essential to conversion. You can readily understand, therefore, that it would be almost an utter impossibility to convert a man whose stomach is crammed with undigested bacon, beans, cabbage, cucumbers, sausages, buttermilk, corn bread, etc., etc. If, then, the candidates eat at all, it should be very sparingly of rice, sweet milk, half-cooked eggs, and other similar articles, and during the entire experiment they should strictly abstain from the use of tobacco and intoxicating drinks.

By strictly observing all these directions, you ought to be able to convert children and nervous women in about three days. Even the toughest old male sinners ought to succumb to this course of treatment within a week. In the good old days, when Methodists were accustomed to worship God with their hearts, when they were accustomed to put themselves under the proper magnetic conditions, their conversions were comparatively easy, and were frequently attended by the trance state, and by clairvoyance. Now, however, since Methodists, like other Christians, have come to worship God with their clothes, their conversions have become comparatively rare and difficult, and are very seldom attended by trance or by clairvoyance.

You now understand how our spiritual faculties may be aroused to action. It is neither by any special merit in any particular religion, nor by the interposition of any particular god. In regard to this matter all religions and all gods are exactly alike. The shouting pagan, the shouting Brahman, the shouting dervish, and the shouting Christian, are all equally happy in the same magnetic condition, which each of them is pleased to call "heartfelt religion." In his ignorance, however, each of these parties imagines that his peculiarly joyful sensations are miraculously produced in him, as a token of love and of approbation, by the direct interposition of his particular god, whom he believes he has succeeded in pleasing, by means of his fastings, his prayers, his sacrifices, etc. Each one of these parties also ignorantly imagines that his is the only god whose followers are thus filled with "joy unspeakable and full of glory." Each one of them, therefore, very naturally, condemns as false all the gods, and all the religions, except their own. From this ignorance arises all the bigotry, all the intolerance, and all the religious persecutions, of the world. Let the truth only be known, and all this bigotry, this intolerance, etc., will cease.

I bring the phenomenon called conversion into this discussion because that phenomenon is simply a magnetic condition which frequently precedes or accompanies clairvoyance, and which is induced by the same means as is the latter phenomenon. By whatever means produced, there is nothing miraculous, nothing specially meritorious, in either conversion or clairvoyance. Neither the one nor the other is any proof of superior goodness on the part of the subject of it, and neither the one nor the other is any proof of the superior excellence of any particular religion, or of the approbation of any particular god. As I have already shown, the gods have nothing at all to do with these phenomena, except as operators use them as objects upon which to fix the thoughts of the subject, and with which to thus arouse him to the proper magnetic condition. In order to succeed well, the operator in all cases should invoke the god in which the subject is a believer. If the prejudices of the subject be shocked, he will not go into the magnetic condition necessary to conversion and to clairvoyance. If, then, the subject be a Brahman, you should, of course, invoke Brahm; if he be a Mussulman, you should invoke Allah, and should bring in the name of Mohammed; if he be a Christian, you should invoke Jehovah, and should bring in the name of Jesus. Remember these things, therefore, in your developing circles, and your revival meetings, and in all cases try to adapt your proceedings to the prejudices of those upon whom you are operating.

The phenomena of conversion and clairvoyance are just as much the results of natural laws as are those of hunger, thirst, sleep or death; and are just as destitute of merit. By supplying the necessary set of natural conditions, any one of these phenomena may be produced at pleasure. Let a man in good health fast about three days, and intense hunger will result. Let him, in connection with the proper mental action, fast about three days longer, and conversion or clairvoyance will result. Let him still fast about three days longer, and death will result. The first of these three phenomena—hunger, and the last, death—are admitted on all sides to be entirely in accordance with the laws of Nature, and to be totally destitute of any merit. So of conversion and clairvoyance, the intermediate phenomena in this experiment. Produced in this case by precisely the same process as are the hunger and the death, they are bound to be just as natural, and just as destitute of merit. The same is equally true of all these phenomena, when produced by any other means.

Let these things be remembered by our religious friends who arrogantly assume that they alone are heirs of heaven, and that all the rest of us are doomed to eternal damnation. Let these persons understand that so far from being a proof that they are better fitted for heaven than are their equally honest but unconverted neighbors, their conversion is simply a proof that they are more nervous than are those neighbors—more susceptible to magnetic influences—more easily made the pliable and profitable instruments of that proverbially cunning and arrogant but totally non-producing class of men who have been the curse of all nations and of all ages— the priests. Let our converted brethren fully understand these facts, and they will cease to be the intolerant bigots that too many of them now are.

I wish it to be distinctly understood that no god has anything to do with the phenomena of conversion, clairvoyance, clairaudience, etc.; that there is nothing peculiarly sacred about them; and that they are just as proper subjects of scientific experimentation as are the penomena of telegraphy and telephonetics, or any other phenomena depending upon the agency of magnetism. Knowing that I regard the matter in this light, you will be able to understand that I do not mean to be either blasphemous or trivial when I suggest that the day may yet come in which conversion and the other phenomena in question may be produced by machinery. Why should they not be thus produced? They are the results of certain causes, and if a magnetic machine could be so constructed as to supply these causes, would not the effects be bound to follow? Start a few converting machines to running, and there is no telling how soon we might be able to convert the whole world.

Remember that success, both in developing circles and in revival meetings, depends entirely upon the presence of certain natural conditions, most of which I have described. If any of these conditions be wanting, complete success is impossible. There can not be an effect without a corresponding cause. Let a spiritual circle be in session, and let the spiritual manifestations be all that could be desired. Then let some sudden and terrible fear seize upon the members of that circle, and these manifestations will instantly cease. The conditions upon which they depend will no longer be present. So of a revival meeting. Let it be in full blast. Let a whole brigade of first-class shouters be all exerting the utmost powers of their lungs and their muscles at once. Then let the cry of "Fire!" reverberate through the church. In an instant every vestige of their joyful feelings will be gone from those shouters, and so far from trusting their God to save them, like frightened sheep they will trample one another to death in their frantic efforts to save themselves. Almost every year this fact is demonstrated anew by some fearful church accident. On such occasions the magnetic conditions are entirely destroyed upon which depends that wonderfully joyful sensation called "heartfelt religion." The sensation of course ceases with the departure of the conditions upon whose presence it depends. The poor shouters then find that neither their God nor their religion is of the slightest use to them in their sudden and fearful danger.

Even very trivial dangers or annoyances are sufficient to destroy the magnetic conditions upon which the joyful sensation in question depends. Any revival can be instantly checked by letting loose among the congregation a few dozen angry hornets or bumblebees. It is utterly impossible for a man to get religion, or even to retain what he has got, while angry hornets and bumblebees are buzzing and bumbling and stinging in his hair, and under his clothes. If you do not believe this, try it. And now, let me ask, if the revival were the work of a god, as is always pretended, could his work be thus stopped by a few hornets or bumblebees?

I now proceed to the consideration of inspiration, the last, and in some respects the highest, phase of spiritual mediumship. This is a purely spiritual phase, and is rather difficult to explain, from the fact that there is no corresponding method of communication in common use among men.

There are two distinct forms of inspiration. In the one of these forms, without the use of language, facts unknown to him are communicated to the medium. In the other form, without any facts being communicated, the medium's mental powers are merely strengthened.

The word inspiration is of Latin derivation, and means a breathing into. In order that you may understand how a spirit, without the use of either words or signs, is enabled to breathe, as it were, into a man thoughts and mental powers, you must understand that every man's brain is the center of a magnetic sphere of greater or less extent, which is pervaded by his own thoughts, and which may also at the same time be pervaded by the thoughts of another. You must also understand that every spirit's brain is likewise the center of an exactly similar magnetic sphere. Finally, you must understand that, like magnetism or electricity, a spirit has power to pervade or take possession of the whole body of a man. The Bible and all history are full of instances in which persons have been thus pervaded or taken possession of by spirits either good or evil.

Now let a spirit, in the manner just described, so permeate or take possession of the body of a man that the center of its brain shall fall upon the center of his. It is evident that like the light from two candles placed near each other, the magnetic or thought sphere of the spirit and that of the man now coincide, or occupy the same space at the same time. It is also equally evident that, so long as this brain union continues, the thoughts of the spirit are all bound to equally pervade the brain of the man, and to become his property. So of the man's thoughts. The spirit obtains possession of them all. This silent and mysterious interchange of thoughts is one form of what we call inspiration. The world has always been filled with persons thus inspired.

Were it not for the physical impossibility of making their brain centers coincide, two living persons could thus mutually inspire each other just as easily as can a man and a spirit. Indeed, even as it is, this form of inspiration does exist in different degrees of perfection among the living. The magnetic or thought spheres of two persons, especially if they differ in sex, and be as unlike as possible in their magnetic conditions, very frequently so unite that the thoughts and the emotions of the one become at the same time the thoughts and the emotions of the other. Indeed, perfect love, the only true marriage, consists in this very union. A man and a woman thus united are truly married without that miserable, meaningless mummery, the marriage ceremony of a priest. Marriage is entirely a natural phenomenon, and none of the operations of nature are ever dependent upon the ceremonies of a priest. Marriage, in its perfection, existed long before priestly ceremonies were invented, or human laws were known. The union of unlike magnetisms in the formation of marriage is no more dependent upon the ceremony of a priest than is the union of oxygen and hydrogen in the formation of water, or that of the primary colors in the formation of solar light. A man and a woman, united, in the manner I have described, by the eternal and unchangeable laws of nature, do indeed become one—one in joy, one in sorrow, one in all the hopes, the fears, and the aspirations of life. Such persons are truly joined together by what you call God, and in no other way does he ever join them together. If, then, a man and a woman be not thus joined together, they are not married, no matter how many priests may have pronounced them man and wife. At best such parties are simply living together in legalized prostitution. It is of the real marriage, the God-made union, and not of the legalized prostitution, that Jesus speaks, when he says: "What therefore God hath joined together, let no man put asunder." He says nothing about what the priest hath joined together. Indeed, as I shall fully show in a future lecture, he wished to protect the true marriage from all human interference. Our marriage laws, as I shall also show in that same lecture, are in direct conflict with this command. They put asunder what God hath joined together.

In the other form of inspiration the spirit, in the same way, pervades with his magnetic or thought force the brain of the man whom he wishes to inspire. In this form, however, mental power alone, and not ready-made thoughts, is communicated. To render this more clear, let us compare the man's brain to a steam box which from a small boiler is supplied with a certain amount of steam. It is evident that this steam box can exert upon the machinery no greater force than itself receives from the boiler. From another boiler, however, let an additional supply of steam be turned into this box, and then, of course, it can exert upon the machinery a force equal to the sum of the forces which it receives from the two boilers. So with the man. His brain being supplied by inspiration, with a stream of thought-force in addition to his own, is enabled, so long as his brain can bear the increased pressure, to perform mental labors far beyond the natural powers of his mind. This form of inspiration is very common. Nearly all the truly grand thoughts ever conceived have been due to its influence. Persons of feeble constitutions, however, should not indulge in this form of inspiration. You can readily understand that by subjecting them to the force of an additional supply of steam, a weak steam box, or weak machinery, might be suddenly destroyed. Let this hint suffice.

Let us now consider the value of that which is communicated or produced by means of inspiration. It is generally assumed that whatever is given by inspiration is, for that reason alone, necessarily true. This assumption, however, as I shall show, is totally destitute of foundation. The facts are that inspired writings, and other inspired communications, are just as liable to be false as are those which are uninspired. All this I will prove.

In the first form of inspiration—that in which ready-made thoughts are communicated—the statements are all the spirit's own, all manufactured in his own brain. Admitting, then, that the inspired person, or medium, be honest, and that he gives us precisely what the spirit gives him, we still have no assurance of the truth of that which is communicated. Its truth depends entirely upon the character for veracity of the spirit that makes the communication. If we know nothing of his character in that respect, his inspired communications, especially if in themselves they be unreasonable, must be set down as at least doubtful. We must remember that a spirit is not necessarily any more truthful than is a man.

In the other form of inspiration—that in which mental power alone is communicated—the statements are all the inspired person's own, all manufactured in his own brain. Their truth, then, depends entirely upon the man's own character for veracity. Inspiration has simply given him an increase of mental power, not, necessarily, an increase of honesty. Indeed, he may be just as truly inspired to tell a lie as to tell the truth. Thus you see that, in no case, is inspiration of itself any proof of the truth of that which is communicated by means of it. Theologians mislead the people in regard to this matter.

For obvious reasons nearly all priests claim that the Bible was given by inspiration of God, and that consequently its teachings must be true. In reply I will say that this is all a barefaced priestly assumption, totally unwarrantable by the facts, and consequently utterly worthless as argument. We have not a particle of proof, either external or internal, that the Bible was given by inspiration at all; and, assuming that it was, we have not a particle of proof that God was the source of that inspiration. Indeed, as I have already shown, we have no proof at all that there is any God. His existence rests entirely upon unwarrantable assumptions.

Assuming, however, that there is such a being, that the writers of the Bible were inspired by him, and that, through the hands of a thousand unknown and uninspired copyists, translators, designing priests, and partisan councils, those writings have reached us uncorrupted, have we still any proof of the truth of those writings? None. Is not the fact that they were given by inspiration of God a positive proof that they are true? Certainly not. Do I call in question God's character for veracity? On my own authority I do not. I know nothing about his character for veracity, or for anything else, except what I learn from the Bible, and from the priests. The Bible, however, does call in question his character for veracity, as well as for most of the other virtues, and clearly shows that in regard to many of them he was certainly most wofully wanting. The Bible, indeed, represents God as a mere magnified reflection of the Jewish leaders, in whose hands he seems first to have made his appearance. Those leaders seem to have made him in their own likeness and image. At any rate, he is represented as being the God of the Jews alone, and as being himself, in all respects, a Jew. Like other Jews of that time, he is represented as being cruel, partial, avaricious, deceitful, revengeful, and unjust; a violator of oaths, an employer and rewarder of liars, a promoter of slavery, of polygamy, of concubinage, of robberies, of wholesale butcheries, etc. This being his character, as given by his own inspired writers, it seems to me that we should regard communications coming from him as at least of doubtful authenticity.

I am aware that I am using very bold language—bolder perhaps than any other public speaker has ever yet dared to use. I am aware that any man, even a monarch, who had dared to use such language at no very distant period in the past, would have perished by the most horrible tortures at the hands of the professed followers of the merciful Jesus. I am aware, too, that almost daily I meet good orthodox Christians who, if they only possessed the power to do so, would at once proceed to experiment upon me with fire because of the expression of my honest religious convictions. As it is, to the full extent of their power they proscribe me in my profession, and strive to render my life one of poverty, of hardships, and of sorrows. And yet I speak nothing but simple truths which ought to be known to the world. In former works I have fully established all I have said, and more, concerning the character of the God of the Bible. As properly connected with the subject of inspiration, I will now briefly examine his character for veracity, and for fair dealing with the inhabitants of earth.

Since, in making this examination, I shall be compelled to come in conflict with some of the life-long and the most fondly cherished religious prejudices of many of my hearers, I wish you to reflect that, however otherwise it may appear from your own standpoint, from mine there is nothing in the least blasphemous, sacrilegious, irreverent, or improper, in the making of such an examination. Reflect that just as Brahm, Josh, Jupiter, or Juggernaut stands to your own candid judgments, so does the God of the Bible stand to mine. Reflect that just as you regard Juggernaut, for instance, so I regard the God of the Bible, as a purely human, and a decidedly hurtful, invention, gotten up by the priests for the purpose of giving themselves power over the ignorant, superstitious, and credulous masses. Reflect that as yourselves, with perfectly proper motives, could enter into an examination of Juggernaut's character, so I, with equally proper motives, can and do enter into an examination of the character of the God of the Bible. Indeed, we differ very little. On the very best of grounds you reject all the gods of the world but one—the one with which you were stuffed before you were old enough to reason, and concerning whom you have never since dared to exercise your reason. On precisely the same grounds I reject that one also, just as you would if, like myself, you dared to make him a subject of investigation, just as you make the other gods.

In Num. xiv, 30, we read: "Doubtless ye shall not come into the land concerning which I sware to make you dwell therein, save Caleb the son of Jephunneh, and Joshua the son of Nun." Here God admits that he had sworn to put the Hebrews, to whom he is speaking, in possession of a certain land or country, to which they were now on their way. Having worked himself up, however, into a towering rage, because the people had believed the reports of certain scouts whom he himself had sent out, he now declares that he will not fulfil his sworn promise; that, so far from leading them into a land of plenty, as he had sworn that he would, he will cause them to miserably perish in the wilderness. The history of this affair shows that he actually did, in direct violation of his sworn promise, carry out this cruel threat.

And now what do you call this wilful failure to fulfil his sworn promise? In the latter part of the thirty-fourth verse we read: " . . . and ye shall know my breach of promise." Since his treacherous act was a breach of promise, and since he himself calls it by that name, dare you call it anything else?

Since God is omniscient, he certainly knew when making the promise in question that he would never fulfil it. Knowing this, he certainly did not intend to fulfil it. He could not have intended to do that which he knew he never would do. Besides this, being himself omnipotent, there was no power in the universe could have prevented him from fulfilling that promise, had he desired and intended to fulfil it. With him, to will was to accomplish. He foresaw all the circumstances of the case, and himself had full control of those circumstances. He foresaw his own breach of promise, and the consequent destruction of the Hebrews in the wilderness. In order to foresee these things, he had, of necessity, to foreordain them. He could not have foreseen, as unchangeable facts in the future, anything except what he himself had determined should be. He alone had the planning of the future. It is evident, then, that he deliberately made a false promise to the Hebrews, and that, when he made that promise, he had treacherously planned their destruction. If, then, he inspired the unknown author of the book of Numbers to write the truth, he himself stands convicted of the very worst form of promise-breaking and unfair dealing. If, however, he inspired that author to write a lie, he himself still stands convicted of wilful falsehood, in thus unnecessarily inspiring the author to write a lie. In any possible view of the case, therefore, your God stands convicted of falsehood and unfair dealing.

In 2 Chron. xviii, 19-22, we read: "And the Lord said, Who shall entice Ahab king of Israel, that he may go up and fall at Ramoth-gilead? And one spake saying after this manner, and another saying after that manner. Then there came out a spirit, and stood before the Lord, and said, I will entice him. And the Lord said unto him, Wherewith? And he said, I will go out and be a lying spirit in the mouth of all his prophets. And the Lord said, Thou shalt entice him, and thou shalt also prevail: go out and do even so. Now, therefore, behold, the Lord hath put a lying spirit in the mouth of these thy prophets, and the Lord hath spoken evil concerning thee." What plans for the enticing of Ahab to his destruction were proposed by God's other advisers we are not informed. We are informed, however, as you see, that God was best pleased to accomplish this object by wholesale and systematic lying, and that he employed an expert in this valuable art to carry out his plans.

In this affair we certainly have an example of genuine spiritual mediumship. A genuine spirit makes genuine, though false, communications through certain genuine mediums called prophets. We also have in this affair another proof that whenever it suits his purpose to do so the God of the Bible is wont to resort to real hard lying. Of necessity, this account is either true or false. If false, then, according to your own teachings, God inspired the unknown author to write a falsehood. If true, then God did resort to the despicable expedient of employing an unblushing liar to lure Ahab and his followers to destruction. These victims of divine lying were God's own children, whom, by simply willing that that they should become so, he could have rendered good and happy men. In any view of the case God stands before us convicted of falsehood and unfair dealing.

In Jer. iv, 10, we read: "Then said I, Ah, Lord God! surely thou hast greatly deceived this people and Jerusalem, saying, Ye shall have peace; whereas the sword reacheth unto the soul." In xx, 7, we also read: "O Lord, thou hast deceived me, and I was deceived." Did God really act the part of a deceiver, as Jeremiah says he did, or did he inspire Jeremiah to write a lie concerning these things? In either case, what kind of a character has God for veracity and fair dealing?

In Ezek. xiv, 9, we read: "And if the prophet be deceived when he hath spoken a thing, I the Lord have deceived that prophet." Did God thus deceive prophets, or did he inspire Ezekiel to write a lie concerning these things? In either case, what kind of a character has God for veracity and fair dealing?

In 2 Thess. ii, 11, 12, we read: "And for this cause God shall send them strong delusion that they should believe a lie: that they all might be damned. . . ." Of necessity, this assertion is either true or false. If it be true, then God actually does furnish certain persons with a lie, and then, with his almighty power, delude them into believing it, and all "for this cause: that they all might be damned." If it be false, then God inspired Paul to write a lie concerning this matter. In either case, what a fearful character it gives God! Can all the theological whitewashers of the world ever render such a being worthy the love and the adoration of good and intelligent men?

Admitting that Paul writes the truth, and that for the sole purpose of thereby devising an excuse to damn them God does thus irresistibly delude certain classes of persons into believing a lie, which, of necessity, he must have ready for them, what proof have our orthodox brethren that they are not the very persons thus deluded, and thus booked for eternal damnation? Would it not be just as fair for him to thus delude them into believing a lie, "that they all might be damned," as it would be for him to thus delude anybody else for the same purpose? Indeed, by reading the whole chapter, you will see that the language in question is certainly not applied to unbelievers. It is true, as we learn elsewhere, that these are to be damned, but their damnation is to be because they have not believed at all, and not because they have believed a lie. Paul describes those to whom he applies the language as sitting in the temple of God, claiming to be the people of God, and arrogating to themselves the powers and prerogatives of God. They were to consist of a portion of the church who should fall away from the church, but who should still be loud professors of religion, while following the false doctrines of their heretical leaders.

The victims, then, of God's "strong delusion" must, of necessity, be looked for inside of some church organization. All theologians admit this fact, and differ only when they come to fix upon the particular sect or division of the church who are to be thus deluded and damned. For obvious reasons no sect fix upon themselves. They think it a very lovely act for God, by means of so treacherous a trick, to thus delude and damn some rival sect, but for him to thus trick and damn themselves they think would be grossly cruel and unfair.

In view of all these things the Protestants claim, and very clearly prove, to their own minds at least, that the Catholics correspond exactly to the description given by Paul of those whom God proposes to delude, and then to damn for being deluded. The Catholics, on the other hand, claim, and just as clearly prove, the same in regard to the Protestants. I suspect that both sects are about right in their views on this subject, and that both will be tricked and damned. Indeed, it seems to me that damnation is a very appropriate fate for those who, with their eyes open, still persist in worshiping a God whose own word proves him to be cruel, partial, treacherous, and unjust. Knowing God's character, these parties should not complain if they are damned. In any view of the case there seems to be very little chance to escape damnation. A great portion of us are to be damned for what we do not believe. A great portion of the balance are to be damned for what they do believe. The religion on which they are depending for salvation is extremely liable to be the very "strong delusion" which God has sent them, "that they might be damned." Let us all, then, prepare for damnation.

These are but a few of a vast number of passages which I might quote, all going to prove that the God of the Bible is by no means always the God of truth. It is true, however, that this same God, as now taught, is a much better being. He has often been remodeled, as I could easily show, and greatly improved, since the communications which I have quoted were made. He is now a magnified reflection of the men of to-day, and is just as much superior to his ancient self as the men of to-day are superior to the men of those ancient times. As men improve, so in all cases do their gods improve.

And now, in conclusion, I will say that I condemn no one for not believing the doctrines which I teach. I leave all such intolerance to the members of the various churches. No man can help either what he believes or what he disbelieves. His will has no control over these things. He believes or he disbelieves a thing, simply because he has no power to do otherwise. For us, therefore, to condemn one another for honest differences of opinion on any subject is exceedingly unreasonable and unjust. Why, then, do you so promptly condemn me as a bad and dangerous man, fit only to be persecuted in this life, and damned in the next, simply because I am totally unable to accept your religious creeds? I am just as sincere in my religious views as any of you can possibly be in yours. Were I a hypocrite, I would profess your religion, because it is popular. All hypocrites profess the popular religion. Nothing but sincerity can bind a man to views so unpopular as are mine. Would you have me as an honest man retain these views, which I do believe, or as a hypocrite adopt your views, which I do not believe?

Besides all this, my views are the results of ten times more study and investigation than most of you have ever devoted to this subject. I have been all over the grounds which you occupy. I fully investigated your creeds, and rejected them with sorrow, only when my reason and my conscience compelled me to reject them. Believing these creeds to be true gold, and wishing to demonstrate that they were so, I subjected them to the proper test for gold. Contrary to my fondest expectations, however, they crumbled to worthless dust in the crucible. Then with unutterable sorrow I abandoned them. In consequence of these long and thorough investigations, I am prepared to judge your doctrines. On the other hand, you have not been over all the grounds which I occupy; you have not thoroughly investigated my doctrines, and hence are not prepared to judge them.

At fifteen years of age I was certainly a sincere believer in the Christian religion. While too young to reason, I had been thoroughly stuffed with it. I had also passed through that joyful magnetic condition called conversion; and had I remained as profoundly ignorant as I then was, I would doubtless have been to-day just as sincere, just as happy a believer in that religion, as I then was. However it may be with others, with me ignorance was absolutely necessary to faith. In spite of my utmost efforts to retain it, my faith departed with the dissipation of my ignorance.

You think it a terrible thing for me to reject your particular God, and your particular religion; and yet you, in the very same way, reject every other god, and every other religion. With the single exception of the God with whom you were stuffed in childhood—the only God concerning whom you have never dared to exercise your reason—we are unanimously agreed that all the gods of the world are priestly impositions upon human ignorance. We are unanimously agreed, too, that for us to worship any of these impositions would be one of the basest forms of hypocrisy and wickedness. With regard to the one remaining God, I have dared to use my reason, and have found him to be, like all the others, a priestly imposition upon human ignorance. For me, therefore, to worship him would be just as basely hypocritical and wicked an act, on my part, as it would be on yours to worship Brahm, Josh, Juggernaut, or any other god in whom you have no faith. And would you have me be thus basely hypocritical and wicked? Convince me that your God is indeed a living reality, and then, and not till then, can I, as a truly conscientious man, bow the knee to him in adoration. If you cannot thus convince me, the fault is not in me; it is in the weakness of your own argument.

Except our own reason and our own conscience, what have we to guide us in regard to these things? And are your reason and your conscience any more to you than mine are to me? If, as you teach, a faithful adherence to the dictates of your own reason and your own conscience in regard to these things be a virtue in you and a passport to heaven, how can the same faithful adherence to the dictates of my own reason and of my own conscience in regard to these things be, as you teach that it is, a crime in me, and a passport to hell?

How came you by your particular God, and your particular religion? Did you examine and compare all the gods and all the religions, and then choose the best? Had the relative merits of the various gods and of the various religions anything to do with the matter? Had you any choice at all? Were you not just as much born to your particular God and to your particular religion as you were to your particular color, and to your particular nationality? Is not the same true of the Hindoos, the Ethiopians, and all others in regard to their respective gods, religions, colors, and nationalities? Are not all men equally born to these things? Are not all stuffed in childhood with the religion of the particular country or community in which they happen to be born? Is the fact that a Hindoo happens to be born to the gods and the religion of Hindostan any proof that those are true gods, and that a true religion? Is the fact that an Ethiopian happens to born to the gods and the religion of Ethiopia any proof that those are true gods, and that a true religion? And is the fact that a European or an American happens to be born to the gods and the religion of Europe and of America any better proof that those are true gods, and that a true religion? If the fortuitous circumstance of your birth be any proof in favor of your gods and your religion, is not the same fortuitous circumstance in his case an equal proof in favor of every other man's gods and every other man's religion? Can you advance a single argument in favor of the genuineness of your gods and of your religion which every other man cannot, with equal force and propriety, advance in favor of his? Had you happened to be born in India or in Ethiopia, and had you been early stuffed, as you certainly would have been, with the gods and the religion of that country, would you not have been just as sincere believers in those gods and in that religion as you now are in the gods, and in the religion, to which you did happen to be born, and with which you did happen to be early stuffed? But in that case would your belief in them have been any proof that those were true gods, and that a true religion? And is your present belief worth any more than your equally sincere belief would have been in that case? Is your belief, adopted without reason or investigation, worth any more than is the belief, adopted in the same way, of the worshiper of some other gods? Think of these things, and learn to be reasonable and just.

NOTE.—In addition to the five phases of Spiritual mediumship of which I have treated in this lecture, there seems to be another form called "Materialization." If this be a genuine phase, it is indisputably the most important phase of all. In regard to this phase, however, I am still only an investigator. As yet I cannot give this to the world as an established phase of Spiritualism.

LECTURE V.

OBJECTIONS TO SPIRITUALISM ANSWERED.

In answering the numerous objections which have been urged against Spiritualism, I shall address my language principally to the members of the various denominations of the Christian Church. I do this simply because it is from these persons that nearly all the objections in question originate. To most of these objections I shall give a double answer. In the first place, I shall show that the objections are not founded on facts, and that, consequently, they do not really exist. In the second place, I shall clearly establish the same, or at least parallel, objections to many of the teachings of the Bible and of the Christian Church. In giving these parallel objections, I shall be almost certain to tread, and rather heavily too, upon the theological corns of many of my tender-footed, if not tender-hearted, orthodox brethren. It would be well for them, therefore, to begin taking up their feet out of my way.

One of the most common, and, as many persons seem to believe, one of the most unanswerable, objections urged against Spiritualism is, that it is all a humbug; that all its manifestations consist merely in "tricks" or "feats of jugglery," performed by the mediums themselves.

This objection is really too absurd to be worthy of a refutation. It is never offered by persons of sufficient intelligence to know what they are talking about. It always comes from the unreasoning rabble, who are equally ignorant of the principles upon which spiritual manifestations depend, and of those upon which feats of legerdemain or jugglery are performed. The all-convincing argument ever used by this class of persons against whatever they do not like is this same hackneyed and unsupported cry of "Humbug!" All intelligent persons know that this same cry may be, and that it has been, raised with equal force against all the spiritual manifestations and other so-called miracles upon which the Christian religion depends, as well as against every science known to man.

Were any answer at all to this silly cry necessary, it would be sufficient to refer to my previous lectures, in which I not only fully established the genuineness of spiritual communications, but also clearly explained the principles upon which they are made. Were any further answer necessary, it would be sufficient to call attention to the well-known fact that a majority of our best mediums are children and uneducated persons, who are totally ignorant of the art of jugglery, and who would be detected in the very first attempt, should they undertake to impose upon an intelligent audience by resorting to trickery of any kind.

It may be said that impostors have been detected among those professing to be spiritual mediums. Certainly, such impostors have been detected, and others of the same kind will doubtless be detected hereafter. The imposition, however, practiced by this class of impostors consists not in being spiritual mediums, but in professing to be such when they are not. When you have detected one of these impostors you have certainly not detected a genuine spiritual medium. Counterfeits have been detected on the best of banks. Indeed, no one ever goes to the trouble of counterfeiting the bills of a worthless bank. When you have detected a counterfeit, however, you have certainly not detected a genuine bill, nor are the genuine bills rendered any the less genuine by such counterfeits. Impostors have been detected among those professing to be Christians. But when you have detected such an impostor have you exposed Christianity? Are true Christians rendered any the less true by such impostors? A traitor was detected among the apostles. But did the detection of that traitor expose all the other apostles as traitors? Benedict Arnold was detected as a traitor to his country. But did his treason make traitors of Washington and of all the other patriots of the Revolution? Indeed, impostors have been detected in all departments of human society. But are any of those departments rendered any the less real, or any the less necessary, by such impostors? Can there, indeed, be a counterfeit without something genuine to be counterfeited? Besides all this, the impostors who have been detected among those professing to be spiritual mediums have never been children or ignorant persons, who would be the most readily detected should they attempt fraud of any kind. In all cases of detection the impostors have been persons of more or less real skill in the practice of deception. Such persons, and such only, trusting in their own skill, have ventured, in the name of Spiritualism, to practice frauds upon the people. The manifestations, too, which these impostors profess to exhibit, are rarely such as are recognized at all by Spiritualism. Instead of simple raps, table-tippings, etc., these impostors almost invariably propose to exhibit some "New and Startling Developments." These impostors are nearly sure, also, to demand money for the seeing of their exhibitions. The imposition, therefore, consists not in the things exhibited, since these do not pertain at all to Spiritualism, but in the abusing of the name of Spiritualism by using it in connection with their infamous frauds. You cannot possibly hold such vile pretenders in more utter detestation than do all true Spiritualists, nor can you be any more willing to expose them.

Another very common and by far more plausible objection urged against Spiritualism is that, unknown perhaps to the mediums, its manifestations are produced simply by human magnetism, and that no spiritual intelligences have anything to do in their production. I once held this view myself, and having become a thorough unbeliever in the immortality of man as an individualized intelligence, I undertook to investigate Spiritualism for the express purpose of exposing it. So far, however, from proving it to be an imposition, as I expected they would, my investigations proved it to be a glorious truth. My unbelief in the immortality of the human spirit, together with many of my strongest materialistic prejudices were overcome. and under the benign, the soul-cheering, the soul-elevating, influences of Spiritualism, I became a better and a happier man. And thus must it be with all who give it so thorough and so fair an investigation. Having in previous lectures already fully answered this objection, I shall now give it only a very brief notice.

Spiritual communications, especially when made by means of physical manifestations, involve a species of telegraphy which, of necessity, depends in part upon the action of magnetism. No intelligent Spiritualist pretends to deny this fact. That the presence of magnetism, however, precludes the participation of spiritual intelligences, in the production of these communications, we all do most emphatically deny. Magnetism alone could never produce an intelligible communication. It is merely the vehicle by means of which such communications are conveyed. In all kinds of magnetic telegraphy there must be, of necessity, an intelligence at each end of the magnetic line. This is a fact too well established to require any proof. No sane man would now contend that because magnetism is involved in their transmission all the communications made by means of the ordinary magnetic telegraph are somehow, unconsciously to himself, produced by the very person that receives them, and that no intelligence at the other end of the line has anything to do in their production. Can you, then, be sure of your own sanity when you set up this very same absurd argument in regard to spiritual telegraphy? Do not the two forms of telegraphy act substantially upon the same principles? When, by means of either of these forms of telegraphy, you receive an intelligible communication, are you not absolutely certain that there is an intelligence, from whom it comes, at the other end of the line? Make it certain, then, that the intelligence in question is not a living man, and do you not make it equally certain that he is a spirit?

The only question that can arise is in regard to the amount of evidence, or of precaution, necessary to render it absolutely certain that the communications are not made by living men. Thousands of the most critical tests, made at different times and at different places, by men distinguished alike for their intelligence, their integrity, and their scientific knowledge, have fully established the fact that communications are received, which, under the circumstances, could not possibly be made by men in the body. I myself have made many such tests. I have not time now to describe these tests, nor would I do so if I had. To you they would constitute only hearsay evidence, and, as I did not myself accept Spiritualism on this this kind of evidence, I will not ask you to thus accept it. If it cannot compel belief, then I have no further use for it. Name your own tests, then, so they be only fair, and any good test medium will assist you in making them. In this way, by the evidence of your own senses, you will be fully convinced of the truth of all I have said.

In concluding this part of my subject I will merely call attention to the fact that the objection under consideration bears with as much force against many of the so-called miracles of the Bible and of the Christian church as it does against what are called spiritual manifestations. Give it, then, all the force you claim for it, and you will ruin your own religion.

You will do this, too, without inflicting any very serious injury upon Spiritualism. You will affect only the lower phases of mediumship, leaving entirely unscathed the higher and more glorious phases, clairvoyance, clairaudience, and inspiration.

A third objection, often urged against Spiritualism, is that many of its manifestations are wanting in dignity—that many of its communications are of a trivial nature. This, however, depends entirely upon what the objectors regard as a want of dignity, and as constituting trivialness. Measured by the standard of these grave and dignified personages, an equally large percentage of all the communications among the living would doubtless prove to be equally wanting in dignity, equally trivial in their nature. And yet, who would think of condemning all intercourse among the living on the ground that in this intercourse many of the communications are wanting in dignity?

In reality, there are in nature no such things as dignity and trivialness. These, like the words largeness and smallness, are merely relative terms applied to qualities, not as they really exist in nature, but as they stand related to some arbitrary standard with which they are contrasted. As the same thing may be very large when contrasted with one object taken as a standard, and very small when contrasted with another, so the same thing may possess great dignity when measured by one standard, and may be very trivial when measured by another. Contrasted with a mustard seed, an apple is very large. Contrasted with a mountain, it is very small. So of the dignity or the trivialness of a thing. It all depends upon the standard by which it is measured. No two men have the same standard by which to determine what is dignified in its nature, and what is trivial. To the dancing master, for instance, certain movements of the body may appear to possess all the elements of dignity, and he may regard the teaching of these movements as a very dignified occupation. To the great military chieftain, however, wholly absorbed in the movements of mighty armies, and in the conducting of battles that cause whole nations to tremble, no profession, perhaps, could be more wanting in dignity than that of the dancing master, and no occupation more trivial than that of the dancers. Objectors would do well to remember these things. They would also do well to remember that the two qualities to which the terms dignity and trivialness are applied are, like the qualities of largeness and smallness, equally natural, equally proper, and equally necessary in the economy of nature.

However things may appear when measured by our arbitrary standards, there is, in nature, nothing really undignified—nothing really trivial. Everything should be measured by its own standard. Measured thus, all things, equally natural, will be found equal in dignity. The gentle zephyr, the sparkling dew-drop, the sports of a child, and the growing of a plant, will then be found just as full of dignity, just as natural, just as proper, and just as necessary, as are the terrible tornado, the mighty ocean, the carnage of a great battle, and the awful quakings of the earth herself. Let each be thus measured by his own standard, and the little busy bee will be found just as full of dignity, just as natural, just as proper, and just as necessary in the economy of nature, as is the mighty elephant, or the monstrous whale. Throughout all the departments of nature, dignity, propriety, and necessity are equally distributed. Unless, then, a thing be a departure from nature, it cannot be wanting in any of these qualities. If it seem to be wanting in any of them, we may be sure that it has been measured by a false standard.

Let us now apply these principles to spiritual communications, and see whether they do, or do not, deserve to be stigmatized as undignified and trivial. In the first place, then, if these communications be genuine—and this you are not now disputing—they demonstrate the immortality of the soul, and this is more than all the dignified religious preaching and writing of the world have ever been able to accomplish. Be their character what it may, the fact that communications do come at all from spiritual intelligences proves beyond all dispute, not only that such intelligences do exist, but also that communications between them and ourselves are possible. And can anything be really trivial which thus so fully establishes the most important of all truths? Was the falling of an apple a trivial thing when it led to the discovery of the true structure of the universe? Had even the most trivial message imaginable from the other shore of death's dark and mysterious river reached me long years ago, and thus demonstrated to me the existence of a life beyond this, I should have been spared the long night of indescribable darkness and infidel despair which helped to render me as you now behold me—a prematurely aged and comparatively feeble man.

Besides all this, are not most of the communications in question from the spirits of men whose communications in this life were usually of an equally trivial nature? Are not the communications, then, just such as we should expect? Are they not just what they should be to be genuine? Have we any reason to believe that death, by some miraculous process, instantaneously confers upon men a great increase of knowledge and dignity? If the communications, professing to come from an ignorant and undignified man, were distinguished for the amount of learning and dignity displayed in them, would any of his friends on earth recognize them as his productions? Is not the case better as it now is? And are not most of these communications as dignified as are the questions which call them forth?

Another reason why we should expect spiritual communications to be just what they are is the fact that they are usually made to spiritual circles whose members, assembled in a social capacity, are far more disposed to indulge in light and merry conversation than they are to engage in the delivering and the hearing of solemn orthodox sermons and dignified orations. This is true of all social gatherings, whether spirits participate in them or not. They are meant for enjoyment, and not for displays of dignity or of eloquence. When spirits attend on such occasions they are usually imbued with the same happy social feeling that pervades the living portion of such assemblies, and whenever they have an opportunity to do so they add to the general enjoyment by making known their presence, and by making those light and merry communications which you stigmatize as trivial. All this is obviously just as it should be. At the meeting of loved ones, long separated by distance or by death, a great display of dignity would be very unnatural and very inappropriate. When serious and dignified communications are needed, and are properly called for from spirits capable of making them, and through mediums capable of conveying them, they are usually received.

You object that communications professing to come from the spirits of some of the greatest men that ever lived are frequently of this same light and trivial nature. Very well. Such communications, from such men, are just as they should be. On social occasions, such as I have described, all the great men of the world have been accustomed to unbend from their usual dignity, and to enter as heartily as any others into the light and merry conversation going on around them. All great men know the immense value of good nonsense at the right time. By its use they are all benefited. If they did not occasionally use it they could not long bear the great weight of their wonderful mental labors. The Demostheneses, the Ciceros, the Patrick Henrys of the world have never been wont to attempt any of their grand displays of eloquence at little social gatherings. Why, then, should you expect their spirits to attempt any such things now, especially when they have to rap out their words, letter by letter, on a table, or communicate them through the organs of speech of an inferior person?

No matter how large a ball may be it cannot be

fired from a gun of smaller caliber than its own. No matter how skilful a musician may be, he cannot display that skill upon a very poor and untuned instrument. The quality of the music, indeed, depends almost as much upon the excellence of the instrument as it does upon the skill of the performer. So the quality of spiritual communications depends almost as much upon the mediums through whom they are sent as they do upon the spirits who send them. Through a young boy, or an unlettered savage, a philosopher could not send, verbally, so dignified a message as he could deliver in person. He would be compelled to adapt his message to the carrying capacity of his messenger. Give him for a messenger, however, one who is also a philosopher, equal to himself, and then his message would not be impaired in its transmission. So let a spirit have for a medium a person in every way equal to himself, and his communications will not be less dignified than were those which he made while yet in the body. Inferior spirits easily find spirits equal to themselves. Their communications, therefore, rarely suffer. Not so, however, with spirits of a very high order. They rarely find mediums equal to themselves, and hence their communications nearly always suffer. Indeed, when they do chance to find mediums through whom they can do themselves justice, you are still no better satisfied. Your cry then is that such mediums are capable of doing all those things of themselves. In any case you condemn the communications. If they be impaired by coming through inferior mediums, you condemn them because of their inferiority. If they be not thus impaired, you condemn them because of their superiority.

I have now shown that, under the circumstances, all spiritual communications are just such as we ought to expect. That which you urge, therefore, as an objection to them is really a strong argument in favor of their genuineness. Impostors, indeed, would never be content to give only these commonplace communications. As I have elsewhere remarked, they nearly always attempt to get off something new and startling.

Having thus fully refuted your charge of trivialness, as applied to Spiritualism, I will now show that this charge bears with far greater force against your own religion. In doing this, I shall not notice the almost innumerable absurdities, obscenities, and trivialities peculiar to each of the various sects into which Christianity is divided. On the contrary, I shall go at once to the Bible, and from it show that, considering the dignity of character which you ascribe to him, your adopted God has made communications to men far more trivial than are any of those which you condemn among Spiritualists. I will make you sorry that you ever named triviality as an objection to Spiritualism. Indeed, I defy you to advance any argument against Spiritualism that cannot with equal force be urged against your own religion.

At one time the Hebrew God, whom you have adopted, turns tailor, dressmaker, and laundryman, and devotes whole chapters of the Bible to a description of the various styles in which the priests' bonnets, petticoats, etc., are to be made, of the various kinds of fringes which they are to have, etc., and how the various articles of clothing are to be cleansed. At another time he turns butcher, cook, and dishwasher, and devotes many other chapters to a description of the manner in which oxen, sheep, goats, etc., are to be butchered; of the various modes in which beef, mutton, etc., are to be cooked and served; of the manner in which the skin, the fat, the suet, the caul, the kidneys, the blood, the feet, the head, the entrails, the heave-shoulder, the heave-breast, etc., are to be disposed of; and, finally, of the manner in which the various kinds of dishes are to be washed. At another time he turns water-wizard, and has Moses walking over the ground, with a rod in his hand, to discover the location of water in the earth. At still another time he becomes a medico-detective, and teaches the priests how to discover the guilt of a woman, charged with adultery, by making her drink dirty water till she bursts open.

You will admit that these communications came through the very best of mediums, and that, consequently, they did not suffer in their transmission. Coming, then, as you claim that they do come, unimpaired, from an infinitely perfect God, these communications should be infinitely perfect in dignity, and in every other excellence. But dare you assert that they possess any such infinite perfections? Dare you undertake to prove that, in dignity or any other excellence, they are superior to the contents of our ordinary fashion-journals, our common cook-books, etc.?

In Ex. xxix, 9-25, we read: "And thou shalt gird them with girdles [Aaron and his sons], and put the bonnets on them. . . . And thou shalt cause a bullock to be brought before the tabernacle of the congregation; and Aaron and his sons shall put their hands upon the head of the bullock. And thou shalt kill the bullock before the Lord by the door of the tabernacle of the congregation. And thou shalt take of the blood of the bullock, and put it upon the horns of the altar with thy finger, and pour all the blood beside the bottom of the altar. And thou shalt take all the fat that covereth the inwards, and the caul that is above the liver, and the two kidneys, and the fat that is upon them, and burn them upon the altar. But the flesh of the bullock, and his skin, and his dung, shalt thou burn with fire without the camp: it is a sin offering. Thou shalt also take one ram: and Aaron and his sons shall put their hands upon the head of the ram. And thou shalt slay the ram, and thou shalt take of his blood, and sprinkle it round about upon the altar. And thou shalt cut the ram in pieces, and wash the inwards of him, and his legs, and put them unto his pieces, and unto his head. And thou shalt burn the whole ram upon the altar: it is a burnt offering unto the Lord: it is a sweet savour, an offering made by fire unto the Lord. And thou shalt take the other ram; and Aaron and his sons shall put their hands upon the head of the ram. Then shalt thou kill the ram, and take of his blood, and put it upon the tip of the right ear of Aaron, and upon the tip of the right ear of his sons, and upon the thumb of their right hand, and upon the great toe of their right foot, and sprinkle the blood upon the altar round about. And thou shalt take of the blood that is upon the altar, and of the anointing oil, and sprinkle it upon Aaron, and upon his garments, and upon his sons, and upon the garments of his sons with him. And he shall be hallowed, and his garments, and his sons, and his sons' garments with him. Also thou shalt take of the ram the fat and the rump, and the fat that covereth the inwards, and the caul above the liver, and the two kidneys, and the fat that is upon them, and the right shoulder: for it is a ram of consecration. And one loaf of bread, and one cake of oiled bread, and one wafer of the basket of the unleavened bread, that is before the Lord. And thou shalt put all in the hands of Aaron, and in the hands of his sons; and shalt wave them for a wave offering before the Lord. And thou shalt receive them of their hands and burn them upon the altar for a burnt offering, for a sweet savour before the Lord: it is an offering made by fire unto the Lord."

Thus I might go on and quote chapter after chapter of such nauseous nonsense, all purporting to come from your adopted God, whom you represent as infinitely superior to any man, or to any human spirit. But are these writings infinitely superior to any human productions, or to any spiritual communications? If not, are they not more undignified for such a God to make than are any of our spiritual communications for a poor, unpretending spirit to make? For our spirits, we claim no wisdom superior to that of men. Indeed, we regard our spirits merely as men, changed in their conditions, but not necessarily rendered either wiser or better by that change. From such beings we should expect very imperfect communications—just such, indeed, as we do actually receive. With your adopted God, however, the case is very different. For him you claim infinite perfection in all things. Should not his communications, then, be infinitely perfect in wisdom, in dignity, and in all other good qualities? Are not they an effect, of which he is the cause? And is not the effect always bound to be exactly as the cause? Can an imperfect effect proceed from a perfect cause? Are those productions of your God, which I have read, in any respect superior to many of the productions of men? If not, can your God then be in any respect superior to those men whose productions are equal or superior to his own? Is it not a universally admitted principle of philosophy that an effect can contain no element not present in the cause? If, then, there be any want of dignity, any imperfection of any kind, in the productions of your God, are you not compelled to admit that he, too, is bound to be equally wanting in dignity, or in some other perfection? Dare you, however, make such an admission? If not, are you not bound to claim that all his productions are infinitely perfect in all good qualities? You are bound to choose one horn or the other of this dilemma. If you choose the one horn, you make your God inferior to many men? If you choose the other horn, and claim that all of your God's productions are infinitely perfect in wisdom, in dignity, etc., what becomes of your charge of trivialness against Spiritualism? If such balderdash as I have quoted from the Bible be infinitely perfect in dignity, can the spiritual communications, of which you complain, be so sadly wanting in dignity as you would have us believe?

Do you not now see that you have placed yourselves in an absurd position? Can you still charge trivialness against spiritual communications which profess to come from poor, imperfect human spirits? And can you, at the same time, make it appear that this wonderful God of yours displayed infinite dignity in coming down and hiding in the top of a mountain, and in devoting many months to the giving of such instructions as I have read to a small tribe of semi-barbarous men? Can you make it appear that he displayed infinite dignity when he entered the lists as a juggler to compete in legerdemain with the magicians of Egypt? When he took up his abode in a small room of the tabernacle in order to regale himself with the savory odors of roast beef; and when he contracted with the Hebrews to pardon a certain amount of sin for a certain amount of various kinds of roast meats?

In addition to the payment of all these articles of food, which in those days this wonderful God of yours always charged for pardoning sins, he also prescribed many other conditions, without the observance of which by the people he either could not or would not pardon their sins. As you already know, one of these conditions was that the priests should have the tips of their right ears, of their right thumbs, and of their right great toes smeared with the blood of a ram. Had this ceremony been entirely omitted, or had the ram's blood been placed upon the left ears, the left thumbs, and left great toes of the priests, this whole plan of salvation would have proved an utter failure, and your wonderful God would have found himself compelled to eternally damn the entire people. The blood, too, as you also know, had to be that of a ram. Had the blood of a ewe, or of any other animal except a ram, been used, it would have possessed no sin-pardoning virtue, and, consequently, in this case, as in the other, the people would all have marched hellwards at once. Coming, as you pretend that it does, from an infinitely dignified God, this roast-beef-and-bloody-big-toe plan of salvation must of necessity be itself, like the source whence it comes, infinitely perfect in dignity. But will you be so kind as to point out wherein consists this infinite perfection? This wonderful plan of salvation was in use by your God before you adopted him—when he was the God of the Hebrews alone. When you adopted him, however, you had him abandon this comparatively harmless plan, and adopt the one which, from time immemorial, had been in use among your pagan ancestors—the unspeakably horrible plan which has him require his own innocent son to be butchered and offered to him as an atoning sacrifice, instead of the roast beef, the ram's blood, etc., of the old plan. This horrible plan, founded thus upon murder, and rendering, as it certainly does, cannibalism a necessity, is the one still in use throughout all Christendom. In a former course of lectures, entitled "Deity Analyzed," I have given this plan a full and fair investigation.

And now, let me ask, what would you say of Spiritualists should they seriously publish to the whole world a book filled with such disgusting balderdash about the blood of rams, the big toes of priests, etc., as that is which fills a large portion of the Bible? Perhaps, however, you are so completely blinded by priestcraft that when reading these things in the Bible you are totally unable to see anything but infinite dignity in all these ridiculous ceremonies. From your earliest childhood you have been so thoroughly stuffed with religious prejudices that you dare not bring your reason and your common sense to bear upon any portion of the contents of the Bible. Let us, therefore, change a few names in some of the verses which I have quoted, and suppose them, with these slight changes, to be the production of a spiritualistic writer. Then, perhaps, you will be able to see them in their true light. The change of names is not made in order to render the passages more ridiculous. No such change could possibly render them more ridiculous than they now are. As I have already intimated, the change is made simply because, upon pure scriptures, you could never bring your reason and common sense to bear:

"And thou shalt gird them with girdles [Aaron Smith and his sons] and put the bonnets on them . . . And thou shalt cause a tom-cat to be brought before the hall of the Spiritualists; and Aaron Smith and his sons shall put their feet upon the tail of the tom-cat. Then shalt thou kill the tom-cat, and take of his blood and put it upon the tip of the nose of Aaron Smith, and upon the tip of the nose of his sons, and upon the thumb of their right hand, and upon the great toe of their right foot. Also thou shalt take of the tom-cat the fat and the rump, and the fat that covereth the inwards, and the caul above the liver, and the two kidneys, and the fat that is upon them, and the tail: for it is a tom-cat of consecration: and one pumpkin pie, and one buckwheat cake sopped in gravy, and one bologna sausage, and one hot loaf out of the bake oven."

And now, how do you like this scripture when it is supposed to come from a Spiritualist? Is it not just as full of dignity as is the original? To those who can, and who dare, think, no further comment is necessary.

In the last six verses of the thirty-third chapter of Exodus we have a dialogue in which Moses asks to see your God's glory. Your God replies that his face is too glorious for a mortal to gaze upon—that no man can behold it and live. He says, however, that he is willing to show his "back parts," which, being far less glorious, can be seen with comparative safety. While getting ready to show the parts named, he holds his hand over the eyes of Moses, lest this clear-sighted old gentleman may get a glimpse of some more glorious parts. When all is ready he takes away his hand, and actually does make an indecent exposure of his nameless "back parts" to the delighted gaze of the morbidly curious, but wonderfully meek, old Moses. In this unspeakably disgusting exhibition of the most indecent portions of his body your God displayed his infinite dignity with a vengeance.

The custom of thus exhibiting only the "back parts" of gods, and of pretending that all their other parts are too glorious to be seen by men, was once quite general, and is said to still exist in Thibet, in Japan, and in some other countries.

In the fourth chapter of Ezekiel we learn that this same God of yours required Ezekiel to lie down on his left side, in full view of the public, and, without turning over, to remain in that position for three hundred and ninety days. At the expiration of this time he was required to turn over and lie on his right side in the same spot for forty days. In order that he might be prepared to make a success of this wonderful stationary exploit he was required to lay in a sufficient quantity of provisions to last him during the entire time. In the ninth verse various ingredients are named which he was to use in making his bread, and in the twelfth verse we read : "And thou shalt eat it as barley cakes, and thou shalt bake it with dung that cometh out of man, in their sight." Ezekiel, however, probably not having a very good appetite, complained that he was somewhat particular in regard to the kind of seasoning which he used in his food, and that the flavor of the article named was a little too strong to suit his fastidious taste. Your God, therefore, willing to humor his fastidious whim, says, in the fifteenth verse : "Lo, I have given thee cow's dung for man's dung, and thou shalt prepare thy bread therewith." This change seems to have exactly suited the taste of the famous old prophet. At any rate, he ate without further complaint the bread made according to your God's last recipe, so kindly given.

And now, let me ask, can you point out any acts, or any teachings, of Spiritualists that equal, in want of dignity, these strange acts and teachings of your adopted God? Have Spiritualists of the male sex ever been so wanting in dignity as to engage in the trivial occupation of putting bonnets and petticoats upon one another? Have Spiritualists ever been so wanting in dignity as to engage in the still more trivial and the totally unnecessary occupation of smearing one another's right ears, right thumbs, and right great toes, with the blood of rams? Have they ever been so disgustingly wanting in dignity, and in decency, as to engage in the trivial, the shameful, occupation of lying down in public places, and remaining there, in the same position, wallowing in their own horrible filth, for more than a year at a time? Have they ever been so wanting in dignity as to engage publicly and ostentatiously in the worse than trivial occupation of feasting upon the unutterably loathsome Ezekiel cake which has been described? Finally, have they ever been so utterly lost to all sense of dignity and of decency as to engage in the abominable act of exhibiting their "back parts" to one another, or to the public?

You cannot deny that your adopted God either did all these things himself, and a thousand more like them, or had them done by his favorite followers. Would it not be well, then, for you to show a little more dignity in his character before you howl so loudly about the want of dignity in Spiritualism? Do you require Spiritualists to be superior in dignity to your God himself? You claim, however, that your God, since you adopted him, has quit all his absurd, his undignified, and his indecent ways. Very well. I am truly glad to hear of his much needed reformation. But how old was he when this reformation took place? Should you not give Spiritualists as much time in which to reform as you gave him? And, if he has thus changed, why do you teach that he is unchangeable?

A fourth objection often urged against Spiritualism

is that it leads to infidelity. In reply to this charge I will say that it depends entirely upon what you mean by the term infidelity. If you mean atheism, then the charge is utterly false. Spiritualism has nothing to do with theology, and a great majority of Spiritualists are believers in the existence of some such being as your adopted God. It is true that many Spiritualists are atheists. Spiritualism, however, had nothing to do in making them so. As well might you argue that agriculture, the mechanical arts, etc., lead to atheism, as to argue that Spiritualism has a tendency to do this. Spiritualism, indeed, has an exactly opposite tendency. By demonstrating that finite spirits do exist it renders more easy the belief that an infinite spirit may exist. Show me one atheist who has become such since embracing Spiritualism, and I will show you a hundred who have become such in the Christian church, or at least under its influences. I am a thorough atheist myself, but I became such while laboring faithfully as an orthodox minister of the gospel, fourteen years before I began the investigation of Spiritualism. With all my intense devotion I found it utterly impossible for me to love, to respect, or even to believe in the existence of so jealous, so cruel, so unjust, so undignified, and so indecent a being as the Bible represents your adopted God as having formerly been. For many years—years of unutterable darkness and despair—I did my best, but in vain, to believe in this monstrous being. I finally came to the conclusion, to which nearly all honest investigators sooner or later come, that your God, like all other gods, is simply an invention with which priests manage to keep the ignorant and superstitious masses in subjection.

If, however, by the term infidelity you mean the manly use of our reason and our common sense, unterrified by priestly denunciations, and absurd creeds, then I freely admit that nearly all Spiritualists are, to a greater or a less extent, tinctured with infidelity. They undeniably do, as a class, rank very high as free thinkers and correct reasoners. It is not so much the embracing of Spiritualism, however, that leads men to become free thinkers and correct reasoners, as it is the exercising of free thought and correct reasoning that leads them to embrace Spiritualism. Persons who either cannot, or dare not, think for themselves, never become either Spiritualists or infidels. Such persons, on faith alone, piously swallow down whatever their priests may see fit to put into their mouths, and, as a natural consequence of such pious compliance, they nearly always die firm believers in the religion with which they happen to have been stuffed, no matter how absurd or degrading that religion may be. For obvious reasons such persons never make any progress. Indeed, founded as it is upon an unchangeable God, and upon an unchangeable book, Christianity itself, if unperverted, is, of necessity, totally incapable of change, of progress, or of improvement. By binding upon us the doctrines of the ancients, by requiring us to worship their system or family of gods, and by holding up their characters and their lives as sacred models for our imitation, it necessarily tends entirely to retrogression. It necessarily tends to lead us back into the darkness, the ignorance, the superstition of the gloomy past, and to shut out the light, the learning, and the mental freedom of the brighter present. Denouncing as the most damnable infidelity all rejections of its doctrines, or of its models, all departures from them, and all advances beyond them, it necessarily tends to keep alive among us the foul principles of slavery, of bigotry, of cruelty, of polygamy, of concubinage, etc., which constitute the most prominent characteristics of its principal God and of its most noted models. It claims that, in thus leading us back into the customs of the times in which these principles prevailed, it is leading us into the simplicity and the innocence with which God is best pleased. It teaches that the farther we go back into the misty distance of the past, the nearer to God we find the people, and that the more we progress, the more we differ from those people, the farther we depart from God, and from the hope of salvation.

All this, as you must plainly perceive, is bound to render the Christian religion the most formidable of all enemies to every form of progress and improvement. And does not the whole history of its course prove that this view is correct? For ten centuries it had full sway over the fairest portions of earth; and because of the universal prevalence of ignorance, of crime, and of wretchedness during their continuance, those ten centuries constitute what are called the "Dark Ages." And what was it that dissipated the darkness of those ages? Certainly not the Christian religion. Darkness could never be dissipated by the same cause that produced it. The Christian Church, with desperate tenacity, clung to that darkness as her own most precious property—

as the only condition under which she could fully flourish. She regarded every attack made upon that darkness as an attack made upon herself. She denounced science as infidelity, and burned scientists as infidels. It was only after her power was partially broken by internal dissensions that infidel science was enabled to terminate that thousand years of darkness—that millennium of the Christian Religion. Every historian knows that what I say is true—that all progress in the useful sciences has been made, not by the Church, but in spite of her most bitter and persistent opposition.

A fifth objection to Spiritualism, and the only one that now remains to be noticed, is that its tendencies are of an immoral nature—that it leads especially to what is commonly, though incorrectly, called free-love; the promiscuous and degrading intercourse with each other of the two sexes. This charge is usually made in so malicious a spirit, and with so utter a disregard for truth, that, were I not a minister of the gospel and opposed to profanity, I should feel myself impelled to brand it as a d—d lie! As it is, I will merely say that it contains not even a shadow of truth. How can it? Does the presence in this life of those who are dearest to us—of our mothers, our sisters, our wives, our daughters of all who are good and pure around us, lead us into immoral habits? Does not their presence tend to preserve us from vice? Does it not tend to make us more pure, more like they are? When their loving voices are forever hushed on earth, when their once brilliant eyes have grown sightless and dim, when their dulled ears have ceased to hear our words of endearment, when their warm hearts have grown motionless and cold, when their icy hands have been crossed upon their pulseless bosoms, when their pale and lifeless forms have been laid to rest in the damp and silent abodes of the dead, and when we have returned to weep in our desolated homes, does the sacred memory of those loved ones, thus lost forever to us on earth, does the fond hope of meeting them in a land of light, in homes of fadeless beauty and nameless bliss—do all these things tend to render us degraded in our natures and immoral in our habits? And when years have passed, when age is coming on us apace, when long-continued grief and intense yearning for our dear ones so long departed have aroused our spiritual senses to action; when we again hear their well-remembered voices; when, with joy unspeakable, we gaze on their love-lit faces and their robes of light, when we hear them tell how fondly they are waiting for us to join them in their lands of beauty and their homes of bliss, can all these things tend to lead us into the practice of immoral habits? As well might you teach that the great ocean is the source of dryness, that the glorious sun is the source of darkness, and that heaven itself is the source of wickedness. If our visitants from heaven lead us astray, how full of sin must heaven itself be!

You assert, however, that many persons who profess to believe in Spiritualism do lead immoral lives. Very well. I admit the truth of your assertion, though I do not admit that Spiritualism is in any way responsible for that immorality. How can Spiritualism be responsible for anything which does not and which can not result from its teachings? I can point out a hundred times as many equally immoral persons who profess to believe in the Christian religion. But do you hold Christianity responsible for their immorality?

Spiritualism simply teaches that our spirit friends can and do communicate with us who are still in the body. Beyond a belief in this doctrine, it has nothing to do with either the opinions or the practices of men. The consequence is that Spiritualists are of all shades of opinion in regard to other doctrines, and of all grades of morality. If a simple belief in the presence of our spirit friends can not lead us into immoral habits, then Spiritualism stands fully vindicated from the foul charge which you have brought against it. Upon this vindication I might safely rest my case. Being an old soldier, however, I am not in the habit of receiving a shot without giving one in return. I propose, therefore, to consider the standing of your party in regard to morality.

In the first place, then, let me ask, do you find immorality prevailing among those who have been reared up entirely under the influences of Spiritualism—among those who have never been tampered with by the advocates of the Christian religion? Do you not, on the contrary, usually find these persons, few though they be, distinguished for the purity of their morals? Who are those Spiritualists with whose immorality you are so greatly offended? Can you, among them all, point out any who have not been members of some branch of the Christian Church, or who have not, at least, been reared up under church influences? Do you not uniformly find that these persons formed their immoral habits before they embraced Spiritualism? Do you not also find nearly every form of their immorality stamped with the trademark of the Church? In charging Spiritualism with immorality, you are like the skunk that first sprinkled some of his own perfumery upon a lion, and then, turning up his nose, as if in great disgust, asked the lion what made him stink. I shall not waste time, however, attacking the vices which prevail among the members of the various churches. As usual, I shall go at once to the Bible and its God, and see what they teach us in regard to morality.

In my last lecture I proved that, whenever it seemed to be to his interest to do so, the God of the Bible unhesitatingly resorted to deception, to promise-breaking, etc. I now propose to prove that he also encouraged, and sometimes even enforced, the practice of polygamy, of concubinage, and of many other customs which you would justly condemn as shockingly immoral if they were encouraged by the advocates of Spiritualism.

In 2 Sam. v, 13, we read: "And David took him more concubines and wives out of Jerusalem, after he was come from Hebron." Previous to this time, as we learn elsewhere, he had a goodly number of those beautiful blessings, and yet, in addition to all of these, and to all of those whom I have just mentioned as being taken by him soon after his arrival in Jerusalem, God made him a present of a whole houseful at once of beautiful women. This fact we learn from 2 Sam. xii, 8, in which we read: "And I gave thee thy master's house, and thy master's wives into thy bosom, and gave thee the house of Israel and of Judah, and if that had been too little, I would moreover have given unto thee such and such things." The women given to David on this occasion were the widows of Saul, who was one of David's fathers-in-law. The women, therefore, were all mothers-in-law to David, until he went in unto them, and by so doing made them his wives. Probably God intended, by means of this transaction, to teach men the proper method of disposing of mothers-in-law. Be this as it may, however, he certainly did intend to show to the world that he was emphatically in favor of the practice of polygamy and concubinage among his followers, and that he was willing to give them any reasonable aid in the carrying out of this practice. David was the king, the head of the nation and of the church, and the acknowledged favorite of God. This great man's example, therefore, in this matter, as well as in all others—except the single affair of Uriah's wife—was, by God's public and unqualified approval, made the highest model for the imitation of the people. As might have been expected, the God-approved example of this illustrious man gave a wonderful impetus to the practice of polygamy and concubinage. Indeed, from that time onward, for many generations, men, among the Jews, seem to have been honored and envied in direct proportion to the number of their wives and concubines.

If you only dared to do so you would promptly deny that God ever did express an unqualified approval of David's polygamy and other immoral practices. Such a denial, however, is rendered impossible by 1 Kings xv, 5, in which we read: "Because David did that which was right in the eyes of the Lord, and turned not aside from anything that he commanded him all the days of his life, save only in the matter of Uriah the Hittite." As things "right in the eyes of the Lord," this certainly includes David's degrading practices of polygamy, of concubinage, of lying, etc., as well as his horrible crimes of maiming horses, by houghing them, and of deliberately murdering the innocent women and children of his benefactors, by tearing them to pieces with saws and harrows, by smothering them in brick-kilns, etc.

And now, let me ask, if all these things were "right in the eyes of the Lord," as they certainly were, when performed by David, his favorite, can they be wrong in his eyes now, when they are performed by holy men, in imitation of his model man, David? If these things were ever "right in the eyes of the Lord," can they be otherwise than right in his eyes now? Does he ever change his opinions in regard to what is right and what is wrong? And can he err in regard to these matters? If he never errs, and never changes his opinions, are not all those things which ever were right in his sight bound to be right now, not only in his sight, but in reality? And can a belief in such a God have any other tendency than that of perverting men's moral natures? Will not men naturally incline to be like the God they worship? Will their morality ever be of a higher type than is his? And, in teaching men to worship a God who favors polygamy, concubinage, and other degrading and criminal practices—in holding up, as models of Godliness for the imitation of all men, the Abrahams, the Jacobs, the Moseses, the Davids—the characters most notorious for polygamy, for concubinage, for lying, for treachery, for robbery, for murder, etc., is not the Bible bound to be a pernicious book, and Christianity a dangerous religion?

Not only did this adopted God of yours, in more ways than one, place his seal of unqualified approbation upon polygamy, concubinage, lying, and other vices, practiced by his chosen people, but he also compelled men, under certain circumstances, to practice them. In Deut. xxv, 5, 6, we read: "If brethren dwell together, and one of them die and leave no child, the wife of the dead shall not marry without unto a stranger; her husband's brother shall go in unto her, and take her to him to wife, and perform the duty of an husband's brother unto her. And it shall be that the first-born which she beareth shall succeed in the name of his brother which is dead, that his name be not put out of Israel." If the deceased husband had no brother, his nearest male kinsman, whether married or single, had to go in unto the widow, and raise up seed unto her deceased husband. If there were many brothers, and all of them but one died, leaving wives but no children, the remaining brother, no matter how many wives he might already have, was bound to take, for wives or concubines, all his widowed sisters-in-law, and by them raise up seed to all his deceased brothers. This compulsory form of polygamy and concubinage, involving no love or preference on either side, enforced even in cases in which the parties to it regarded each other with absolute loathing, and having reference to nothing except breeding, as among cattle, was the most degrading of all forms of those abominable practices. And yet this form of brutish breeding was so pleasing to the eyes of your God that he compelled men to practice it.

In the thirty-first chapter of Numbers we have an account of the destruction of the Midianites by an army of Hebrews that Moses, acting under your God's command, had sent out for that purpose. The men of Midian were all slain, but the women and children were all brought in alive as captives. When the victorious army of the Hebrews, with their captives and other spoils, drew near, Moses and the other principal men of Israel went forth to meet them. Then, as we learn from the fourteenth to eighteenth verses, "Moses was wroth with the officers of the host, with the captains over thousands and the captains over hundreds, which came from the battle. And Moses said unto them, Have ye saved all the women alive? . . . Now, therefore, kill every male among the little ones, and kill every woman that hath known man by lying with him. But all the women children that have not known a man by lying with him keep alive for yourselves." These horrible orders were immediately executed.

And now, let me ask, what would you think of your God's conduct should he conclude to have us all slain, our houses all pillaged and burned, our wives, our mothers, our married sisters, and our married daughters, together with our little boys, all butchered in cold blood, while our virgin daughters and our virgin sisters were divided out to sate the brutal lust of the inhuman butchers whom he had chosen as his special favorites? Would he, for such horrible deeds, merit the praises of all men? And yet would he act any worse in treating us and our loved ones in this way than he did act when he treated the Midianites and their families in the same way? For no crime but that of being males, he had those poor little babes torn from the arms of their fond mothers, and their heads crushed by the tens of thousands at once. For no other crime than that of being wives and mothers, he had an immense multiude of poor, helpless women butchered in cold blood. Finally, for no other crime than that of being virgins, destitute of protectors, he divided out 32,000 young girls to be outraged by the brutal soldiery, and the equally brutal priests and other holy men. As for me, I can neither love nor serve such a God. In a published poem, "The Devil's Defense," I have given a vivid description of this and other unutterably horrid scenes enacted by your God's express command:

> " The Lord is a man of war, 'tis said,
>   ' A fierce, a consuming fire ;'
> And countless hosts of the ghastly dead
>   Bear proof of his terrible ire.
> He doth not pity, he doth not spare,
>   He cruelly doth destroy ;
> He doth not care for the wailing prayer ;—
>   To him 'tis a source of joy.
> He ordereth his band, with a bloody hand,
>   To butcher both young and old—
> To render the land like a waste of sand
>   Where the billows once have rolled.
> They haste to obey what their Lord doth command ;
> Like devils incarnate, they waste the whole land.

Alas! for their victims! wherever they turn,
Destruction awaits, while their villages burn.
Dense volumes of smoke, like a vast floating pall,
Hang dark o'er the valley, the mountain, and all.
From the depths of their darkness arise on the air
Such yells of fierce rage, and such screams of despair,
That even the raving of devils in hell
Could never this scene, in its horrors, excel.
By legions the bravest defenders are slain,
Their bodies lie scattered all over the plain;
The few who survive them, like lions at bay,
Now turn on their murd'rers; they yell and they slay;
But, beaten by numbers, their eyes gleaming fire,
They scream their defiance, they fall, they expire.
Of the strong and the brave, the last one is now dead,
And to those who are helpless the carnage is spread;—
There burst forth anew on the smoke-burdened air
More terrible wailings of utter despair;
Old women, whose locks are as white as the snow,
Are butchered and left to be food for the crow;
The poor mothers flee with their babes at the breast;
Oh! could they save these, they'd endure all the rest;
But your God's servants meet them, then round them there rains
A shower of blood mixed with their babies' crushed brains.
Oh! horrible! horrible! maddening sight!
'Twould touch e'en the hearts of the demons of night.

But pity—no pity God's minions do feel,
While mangling those poor little babies with steel.
The fond mothers cling to the bodies yet hot,
They gaze in the eyes, but are recognized not.
The lips that so lately were wreathed in a smile,
All mangled and gory, still quiver a while;
Death's pallor creeps over each sweet little face,
The heart becomes still, and the eyes glaze apace.
The mothers see this, and are now glad to die;
They struggle no longer, no longer they cry;
Their throats are now cut, and their blood, like a
      spout,
On their babies' dead faces, comes gushing right out;
Their bodies, unburied, encumber the sod,
And this all done by your orthodox God."

If it were only in your power to do so, how gladly would you deny that your God was ever guilty of murders so unutterably foul! This denial, however, you cannot possibly make. The Bible is too explicit on the subject. It is too explicit also in regard to the purpose for which the virgin girls were preserved alive. That purpose was one of the foulest of which the human mind can conceive, and yet that purpose was approved by your God. Those pure young girls were preserved for the sole purpose of being outraged by the brutal murderers of their parents, of their baby brothers, of all their loved ones. The language does not admit of any other interpretation. If, as you would like to have it appear, those girls were spared for servants, why were the boys all slain? Would not these have made better servants, especially for the soldiers? And why were all the women slain who had ever been married? Would the fact that they had been wives have rendered them any the less valuable as servants? The case is too plain to require further argument. For sexual purposes alone would the notoriously libidinous Hebrews have been so careful to spare none but women who had never been defiled by the touch of idolatrous men. And, admitting that those young women were preserved ostensibly for servants, how much better does it render the case? To what use did Abraham, Jacob, and all the other Hebrews, so far as we know, put their female servants? What were their female servants, as a rule, but concubines? In this case, there were only 12,000 soldiers, and yet they received 16,000 young women. This would give one woman to each private, and at least a dozen to each officer. And do you pretend that the soldiers and officers had need of so many women as ordinary servants? In any view of the case, how revolting to every sense of modesty was the examination which, through his agent Moses, your God required the soldiers to make of the women, in order to ascertain which ones of them had, and which ones had not, "known a man by lying with him?" How would our good orthodox women of the present time like it if their God should conclude to have them treated in that same manner? Would they still shout his praises? If not, why do you shout his praises at all? Is he not just as guilty now as he would be in that case? In what respect would it be worse for him to have our own women thus outraged, than it was to have the same things done to the women of Midian?

In Hosea i, 2, 3, we read: "And the Lord said to

Hosea, Go, take unto thee a wife of whoredoms, and children of whoredoms: . . . So he went and took Gomer, the daughter of Diblaim; which conceived and bare him a son." Further on, we learn that she bore him two other children; that he then grew tired of her, called her by foul names, threatened to strip her naked in the streets, etc. In ii, 2-4, we read: "Plead with your mother, plead; for she is not my wife, neither am I her husband: . . . And I will not have mercy upon her children; for they be the children of whoredoms." These were his own children by Gomer, the lewd woman, with whom, by your God's orders, he had been cohabiting without even a pretense of marriage.

Having driven Gomer and her children from him, this holy man was prepared to serve the Lord in the bed of another woman of the same character. This we learn from iii, 1-3, in which we read: "Then said the Lord unto me, Go yet, love a woman beloved of her friend, yet an adulteress. . . . So I bought her to me for fifteen pieces of silver, and for an homer of barley, and an half homer of barley. And I said unto her, Thou shalt abide for me many days; thou shalt not play the harlot, and thou shalt not be for another man: so will I also be for thee." With what refreshing simplicity this godly old rake tells us how much he paid as fees to this prostitute, and that, by paying in advance, he had her all to himself for "many days!" When about to engage in similar enterprises, the holy men of our own time would do well to follow Hosea's prudent example.

And now, how do you like your adopted God's morality as exhibited in his repeated instructions to his beloved Hosea? Should you blame the holy men of the present time who attempt to follow the godly example of men so righteous and so favored of God as were Abraham, Jacob, David, Hosea, and others? Are not the lives and the characters of these holy men of the Bible given to us as models? If so, should we not imitate them? Did not your God beget his only son upon an unmarried woman? And are we to condemn or to imitate your God's example? These are only a few of a vast number of examples which I could give, all of which go to show a similar state of morals on the part of your adopted God, and of those who, as models for the world, were acting directly under his instructions.

And now, in conclusion, let me ask, how can such teachings, how can such models, be otherwise than degrading in their influence upon the moral natures of those who accept them as coming from God himself? You teach that this God is utterly unchangeable. Admitting that he is so, is he not bound to see polygamy, concubinage, etc., in the same light to-day as that in which he saw them when he was engaged in encouraging, aiding, and even compelling his chosen people to practice them? According to his own declaration, these practices were then right in his sight. How, then, without a change on his part, must they appear in his sight to-day?

You also teach that all your morality comes from this unchangeable God, as its fountain head. And can a stream rise above its source? Can your morality ever become of a higher type than is that of the God from whom you derive it? Can your morality ever become of a higher type than was that of your Bible models, Abraham, Jacob, Hosea, and others? Dare you say that you are better than were these men? Did they not live farther up the stream, nearer to God, the source, than do you? If, then, your lives be any purer than were the lives of David, Hosea, and other holy men of the Bible, does not that greater purity come from your getting farther away from the God of the Bible?

Finally, are polygamy, concubinage, deception, the butchering of infants, etc., right, or are they wrong? They are bound to be the one or the other. If you say that they are right, what kind of morality do you teach? If you say that they are wrong, what kind of a character do you give to your God who favored these things, and often compelled men to practice them? Has your God reformed, and become better than he was then? If so, when did he reform, and why do you teach that he is unchangeable? You delight to harp upon the purer morality said to have been taught and practiced by Jesus. These harpings, however, can be of no possible service to you in the present discussion. I have not a word to say against the morality imputed to Jesus; but what was he—a God or a man? If a God, was he not this same God? And could he be any better than himself? You may say that he was only God's son, and not God himself. Very well. Then we have two distinct Gods—the Father and the Son. But dare you say that the Son was any better than the Father? If not, what have you gained by bringing the Son into the discussion? If Jesus was only a man, dare you say that he taught and practiced a purer morality than did God himself? Escape these dilemmas, answer these arguments, and then, with much better grace, you can attack the glorious doctrines of Spiritualism. With these remarks, my arguments close.

And now, in conclusion, I will say that when I was entering upon the preparation of this course of lectures, I was well aware that I was entering upon a work which would inevitably bring upon me the unrelenting persecutions of the mighty armies of so-called orthodox theology. Believing, however, that the work was a great and good one, I was willing to bear the persecutions which I knew it would bring upon me. I have borne them, and still continue to bear them. They move me not. Why should they? I am growing old. Years, and toils, and sorrows are deepening the furrows on my face, and the silver hairs are fast crowding the black from my temples. The sun of my life has long since passed its zenith, and is now fast hastening adown to the western horizon. My lengthening shadow now falls entirely behind me. Before me, over the great ocean of futurity, all things lie enwrapped in the glorious radiance of living light. My journey is almost ended; my work is almost done. Soon to the land of the leal will I go, to join my spirit friends, my parents, my sisters, my children, my loved ones all, who have waited for me so long, and who, as ministering angels, sometimes come to me, even now, in their robes of snow, on their wings of light. By far the greater portion of those I have loved have already reached the farther shore of the mystic river, and are dwelling amid the untold beauties of the spirits' Summer-land. Let the change called death, then, come when it may; I am ready; and, as I have lived, so will I die—a man.

COL. JOHN R. KELSO'S WORKS.

THE BIBLE ANALYZED.

Cloth, octavo, 833 pages, - - - - - $3.00

DEITY ANALYZED AND THE DEVIL'S DEFENSE.

Cloth, 12mo., 466 pages, - - - - - $1.50

THE REAL BLASPHEMERS.

Paper, 12mo, 138 pages, - - - - - .50c.

SPIRITUALISM SUSTAINED.

Cloth, 12mo, 245 pages, - - - $1.00.

TRUTH SEEKER OFFICE, 33 Clinton Place, New York.

WORKS BY J. E. REMSBURG.

False Claims. Revised and Enlarged. As a Missionary Document it is unexcelled. Among the subjects considered by Mr. Remsburg are: The Church and Morality; Criminal Statistics, showing the creeds of the prisoners in the penitentiaries; the Church and Civilization; the Church and Science; the Church and Learning; the Church and Liberty; the Church and the Antislavery Reform; the Woman's Rights Movement; the Temperance Reform; the Church and the Republic. Price, 10 cents singly; 75 cents per dozen.

Bible Morals. Twenty Crimes and Vices Sanctioned by Scripture; Falsehood and Deception; Cheating; Theft and Robbery; Adultery and Prostitution; Murder; Wars of Conquest and Extermination; Despotism; Intolerance and Persecution; Injustice to Woman; Unkindness to Children; Cruelty to Animals; Human Sacrifices; Cannibalism; Witchcraft; Slavery; Polygamy; Intemperance; Poverty and Vagrancy; Ignorance and Idiocy; Obscenity. Price, single copies, 25 cents; 6 copies, $1. Special discount on larger quantities.

Sabbath-Breaking. This is the best and most thorough work ever written on the Sabbath from a rational point of view. Large and handsome print. The question is discussed under the following heads: Origin of the Sabbatic Idea; the Jewish Sabbath; the Christian Scriptures and the Sabbath; Examination of Sunday Arguments; Origin of Christian Sabbath; Testimony of the Christian Fathers; the Sabbath during the Middle Ages; the Puritan Sabbath; Testimony of Christian Reformers, Scholars, and Divines; Abrogation of Sunday Laws. Price, 25 cents; six copies, $1.

Image Breaker. Six Lectures: Decline of Faith, Protestant Intolerance, Washington an Unbeliever; Jefferson an Unbeliever; Paine and Wesley; Christian Sabbath. Each 5 cents; bound, paper, 25 cents; per doz. 40 cents.

Thomas Paine. Tells the story of the Author-Hero's life, delineates the leading traits of his character and genius, and vindicates his name from the aspersions cast upon it. Choice extracts from "Common Sense," "American Crisis," "Rights of Man," and "Age of Reason," are given; also, tributes to Paine's character from more than one hundred noted persons of Europe and America many of them written expressly for this work. Second edition, 160 pages, printed on fine tinted paper, neatly bound, and containing a handsome steel portrait of Paine. Paper, 50 cts; cloth, 75 cts.

The Apostle of Liberty. An address delivered in Paine Hall, before the N. E. Freethinkers' Convention, January 29, 1884. Price, 10 cents.

For all the above works address THE TRUTH SEEKER CO., 33 Clinton Place, New York.

PAINE'S WORKS.

Paine's Theological Works, including The Age of Reason, Examination of Prophecies, Letter to the Bishop of Llandaff, Reply to Mr. Erskine, Letter to Camille Jordan, etc., etc., with a life of Paine and a steel-plate portrait. 12mo. In paper covers, $1; cloth, $1.50.

Paine's Great Works (complete) in one volume. Cloth, $3.00; leather, $4.00; morocco, $4.50.

Paine's Political Works, including Common Sense, The Crisis, and Rights of Man. Cloth, $1.50.

The Age of Reason. An investigation of true and fabulous theology. Without a peer in the world. Paper, 25 cents, or 5 for $1. Cloth, 50 cents.

The Age of Reason and An Examination of the Prophecies. Paper, 40 cents; Cloth, 75 cents.

Common Sense. Paine's first work. 15 cents.

The Crisis. Containing numbers from I. to XVI. inclusive. Paper, 40 cents; cloth, 75 cents.

The Rights of Man. For the oppressed of humanity. Paper, 40; cloth, 75 cents.

Paine's Life, with Remarks on Comte and Rousseau. By CALVIN BLANCHARD. Paper, 50 cents; cloth, 75 cents.

B. F. UNDERWOOD'S WORKS.

Essays and Lectures. Embracing Influence of Christianity on Civilization; Christianity and Materialism; What Liberalism offers in Place of Christianity; Scientific Materialism; Woman; Spiritualism from a Materialistic Standpoint; Paine the Political and Religious Reformer; Materialism and Crime; Will the Coming Man Worship God? Crimes and Cruelties of Christianity; the Authority of the Bible; Freethought Judged by its Fruits; Our Ideas of God. 300 pp., paper, 60 cents; cloth, $1.

Influence of Christianity upon Civilization. 25 cents.

Christianity and Materialism. 15 cents.

What Liberalism Offers in Place of Christianity.
10 cents.

Scientific Materialism: Its Meaning and Tendency.
10 cents.

Spiritualism from a Materialistic Standpoint. 10 cents.

Paine the Political and Religious Reformer. 10 cents.

Woman: Her Past and Present: Her Rights and Wrongs. 10 cents.

Materialism and Crime. 10 cents.

Will the Coming Man Worship God? 10 cents.

Crimes and Cruelties of Christianity. 10 cents.

Twelve Tracts. Scientific and Theological. 20 cents.

Burgess-Underwood Debate. A four day's debate between B. F. UNDERWOOD and PROF. O. A. BURGESS, President of the Northwestern Christian University, Indianapolis, Ind. Accurately reported. 188 pp. Paper, 50 cents; cloth, 80 cents.

Underwood-Marples Debate. A four nights' debate between B. F. UNDERWOOD and REV. JOHN MARPLES. Fully reported. Paper, 35 cents; cloth, 60 cents.

MISCELLANEOUS

Freethought Works Published by D. M. Bennett.

A Business Man's Social and Religious Views. Bold and trenchant blows againsts theology and inhumanity. $1.

Advancement of Science. The Inaugural Address of Prof. JOHN TYNDALL delivered before the British Association for the Advancement of Science. With Portrait and Biographical sketch. Also containing opinions of Prof. H. HELMHOLTZ and articles of Prof. TYNDALL and Sir HENRY THOMPSON on prayer. Price, cloth, 50 cents; paper, 25 cents. Inaugural Address alone, in paper, 10 cents.

Alamontada the Galley-Slave. Translated from the German of Zschokke by IRA G. MOSHER, L.L.B. A deeply philosophical narrative, intensely interesting. Price, cloth, 75 cents; paper, 50 cents.

Amberley's Life of Jesus. His character and doctrine. From the Analysis of Religious Belief. By Viscount Amberley. Paper, 35 cents; cloth, 60 cents.

Beyond the Veil. Claimed to be dictated by the spirit of Paschal Beverly Randolph, aided by Emanuel Swedenborg, through the mediumship of Mrs. Frances H. McDougall and Mrs. Luna Hutchinson, with a steel engraving of Randolph. $1.50

Blakeman's 200 Poetical Riddles. 20 cents.

Career of Religious Ideas; Their Ultimate the Religion of Science. By Hudson Tuttle. Paper, 50 cents; cloth, 75 cents.

Chronicles of Simon Christianus. His manifold and wonderful adventures in the Land of Cosmos. A new scripture (evidently inspired) discovered by I. N. Fidel. From the English. Very rich. 25 cents.

Crimes of Preachers in the United States. By M. E. Billings. Shows how thick and fast the godly have fallen from grace. Price, 25 cents.

Deity Analyzed and the Devil's Defense. In Six Lectures by Col. John R. Kelso, A.M. These are among the ablest lectures ever delivered, and should be read by everybody. Price, $1.50.

Ecce Diabolus; or, The Worship of Yahveh or Jehovah shown to be the Worship of the Devil, with observations on the horrible and cruel ordinance of Devil Worship, to wit, Bloody Sacrifices and Burnt Offerings. By the Very Rev. Evan Davies (Myfyr Morganwg), D.D., L.L.D., Arch-Druid of Great Britain. Translated from the Welsh by Morion, B. C. Price, 25 cents.

Eight Scientific Tracts. 20 cents.

Gottlieb: His Life. A Romance of earth, heaven, and hell. Beautifully written, by S. P. Putnam. 25 cents.

Hereafter. A scientific, phenomenal, and biblical demonstration of a future life. By D. W. Hull. Paper, 50 cents; cloth, 75 cents.

Issues of the Age. Consequences involved in modern thought. A work showing much study and great familiarity with other writers and thinkers. By Henry C. Pedder. Price $1.

Jesus Christ. His life, miracles, deity, teachings, and imperfections. By W. S. Bell. 25 cents.

John's Way. A pleasing domestic Radical story. By By Mrs. E. D. Slenker. 15 cents.

Last Will and Testament of Jean Meslier, a curate of a Roman church in France, containing the best of his writings. 25 cents.

Nathaniel Vaughan. A radical novel of marked ability. By Frederika Macdonald. 404 pages. Price reduced to $1.25.

Nature's Revelations of Character; or Physiognomy Illustrated. The science of individual traits portrayed by the temperaments and features. Illustrated by 260 wood cuts. By Joseph Simms, M.D. 650 pages, 8vo. Cloth, $3.00; leather, $4.00; morocco, gilt edges, $4.50.

New England and the People up There. A humorous Lecture. By George E. Macdonald. 10 cents.

Outline of the French Revolution: Its Causes and Results. A clear and comprehensive portrayal of this interesting portion of human history. By W. S. Bell. 25 cents.

Outlines of Phrenology. By F. E. Aspinwall, M.D. Most acceptable to Liberals of anything of the kind published. Paper, 50 cents; cloth, 75 cents.

Pocket Theology. By Voltaire. Comprising terse, witty, and sarcastic definitions of the terms used in theology. The only edition in English. 25 cents.

Proceedings and Adresses at the Watkins Convention. 400 pages of excellent Speeches and Essays. Price reduced to $1.00.

Pyramid of Gizeh. The Relation of Ancient Egyptian Civilization to the Hebrew Narrative in Genesis and Exodus and the Relative Claims of Moses and the Pyramid to Inspiration Considered. By Van Buren Denslow, L.L.D. Price, 25 cents.

Religion Not History. An able examination of the Morals and Theology of the New Testament. By Prof. F. W. Newman, of the London University. 25 cents.

IRON-CLAD AND MANNA SERIES.
Iron-Clad Series.

Atonement. Charles Bradlaugh	5
Secular Responsibility. G. J. Holyoake	5
Buddhist Nihilism. Prof. Max Muller	10
Religion of Inhumanity. F. Harrison	20
Relation of Witchcraft to Religion. Lyall	15
Essay on Miracles. David Hume	10
Land Question. Charles Bradlaugh	5
Were Adam and Eve Our First Parents? Charles Bradlaugh	5
Why Do Men Starve? Charles Bradlaugh	5
Logic of Life, Deduced from the Principle of Freethought. G. J. Holyoake	10
A Plea for Atheism. Charles Bradlaugh	10
Large or Small Families? A. Holyoake	5
Superstition Displayed, with a Letter of Wm. Pitt. Austin Holyoake	5
Defense of Secular Principles. Chas. Watts	5
Is the Bible Reliable? Charles Watts	5
The Christian Deity. Charles Watts	5
Moral Value of the Bible. Chas. Watts	5
Freethought and Modern Progress. C. Watts	5
Christianity: Its Nature and Influence on Civilization. Chas. Watts	5
Thoughts on Atheism. A. Holyoake	5
Is There a Moral Governor of the Universe? A. Holyoake	5
Philosophy of Secularism. C. Watts	5
Has Man a Soul? Charles Bradlaugh	5
Is There a God? Charles Bradlaugh	5
Labor's Prayer. Charles Bradlaugh	5
Poverty; Its Cause and Cure. M. G. H	10
Science and Bible Antagonistic. C. Watts	5
Christian Scheme of Redemption. Charles Watts	5
Logic of Death; or, Why Should the Atheist Fear to Die? G. J. Holyoake	10
Poverty; Its effects on the Political Condition of the People. Charles Bradlaugh	5

Manna Series.

New Life of David. Charles Bradlaugh	5
200 Questions Without Answers	5
Dialogue Between a Christian Missionary and a Chinese Mandarin	10
Queries Submitted to the Bench of Bishops by a Weak but Zealous Christian	10
Search After Heaven and Hell. A. Holyoake	5

New Life of Jonah. Charles Bradlaugh. . . . 5
A Few Words About the Devil. Charles Bradlaugh. . . 5
New Life of Jacob. Charles Bradlaugh. . . . 5
Daniel the Dreamer. A. Holyoake. . . . 10
Specimen of the Bible. Esther. A. Holyoake. . . 10
Acts of the Apostles, A Farce. A. Holyoake. . . 10
Ludicrous Aspects of Christianity. A. Holyoake. . . 10
Twelve Apostles. Charles Bradlaugh. . . . 5
Who Was Jesus Christ? Charles Bradlaugh. . . . 5
What Did Jesus Teach? Charles Bradlaugh. . . 5
New Life of Abraham. Charles Bradlaugh. . . . 5
New Life of Moses. Charles Bradlaugh. . . . 5

RECENT PUBLICATIONS.

AMERICAN SECULAR UNION: Its Necessity and the Justice of its Demands. By Charles Watts. 10c.

BIBLE ANALYZED. By John R. Kelso, A.M. 8vo, 833pp., silk cloth, beveled edges. $3.

BIBLE FABRICATIONS REFUTED AND ITS ERRORS EXPOSED. By O. B. Whitford, M.D. 15c.

BIBLE MORALS: Twenty Crimes and Vices Sanctioned by Scripture. By John E. Remsburg. 25c.

CHRISTIANITY A REWARD FOR CRIME. Authenticated by the Bible. By O. B. Whitford, M.D. 10c.

RATIONAL COMMUNISM. Present and Future Republic of North America. By a Capitalist. Advocates associate life and employment as a preventive of poverty, vice, crime, etc. 12mo, 498p. $1.50.

RELIGION OF HUMANITY BETTER THAN ETERNAL PUNISHMENT. By M. Babcock. 10c.

SABBATH-BREAKING. By John E. Remsburg. 25c.

ST. MATTHEW BEFORE THE COURT FOR THE CRIME OF FORGERY. By Secularist. 10c.

SECULARISM, DESTRUCTIVE AND CONSTRUCTIVE. By Charles Watts. 10c.

SOCIAL WEALTH. The Sole Factors and Exact Ratios in its Acquirement and Apportionment. By J. K. Ingalls. 12mo, 320pp. $1.

THE STORY HOUR. For Children and Youth. By Susan H. Wixon. A series of stories void of the superstitious taint that is contained in most juvenile books of the day. Interesting and instructive to both old and young. Illustrated by nearly 100 beautiful engravings. 4to, 224pp. Bds. $1.25.

TRUTH SEEKER ANNUAL for 1886. Containing Portraits of Leading European and Continental Freethinkers. 8vo, pap. 25c.

MAN; WHENCE AND WHITHER. By R. D. Westbrook, D.D., LL.D. Cloth, $1.00.

MARRIAGE AND DIVORCE. R. D. Westbrook, D.D., LL.D. 50 c.

POSITIVIST'S PRAYER. By Jos. Longchampt. Paper, 25 cts.

PRIMORDIAL PRINCIPLES of the Universe. By C. E. Townsend. 292 pp., cloth, $1.50.

PROBLEMS OF THE UNIVERSE, by S. P. Putnam. Paper, 20 cts.

RECONSTRUCTION OF SOCIETY, by Louis Masquerier. $1.00

RELIGION THE GIBRALTAR OF THE WORLD, by Geo. T. Bondies. Paper, 25 cts.

RIGHTS OF WOMAN, by Ray D. Chapman. Paper, 25 cts.

ROMAN CATHOLIC CANARD. Paper, 10 cts.

SAKYA BUDDHA. A Versified Annotated Version of His Life and Teachings. Cloth, $1.00.

SECRETS OF BEE-KEEPING, by K. P. KIDDER. Boards, 75 cts.

SECRET OF THE EAST, or, THE ORIGIN OF THE CHRISTIAN RELIGION, by Felix L. Oswald, M. D. Cloth, $1.00.

SOUL PROBLEMS—Theological Amendment and State Personality, by Jos. E. Peck. Paper, 25 cents.

SPIRITUAL DELUSION, by D. D. Lum. Cloth, $1.50.

SUBSTANTIALISM, OR PHILOSOPHY OF KNOWLEDGE, by Jean Story. Cloth, $1.50.

SUGGESTIVE THOUGHTS. Cloth, 50 cents.

SUNDAY LAWS, by J. G. Hertwig. Paper, 10 cents.

THERAPEUTÆ, by Geo. Reber. Cloth, $1 00.

TRUTH, A POEM IN FOUR PARTS, by E. N. Kingsley. Paper, 20 cents.

TRUTH SEEKER ANNUAL AND FREETHINKERS' ALMANAC for 1884. 18 full-page ill., 8vo. 116 pp. Paper, 25 cents.

TRUTH SEEKER ANNUAL, for 1885, (ready in December '84), 25 cents.

ULTIMATE GENERALIZATION, An Effort in the Philosophy of Science. Cloth, 50 cents.

WAIFS AND WANDERINGS. A Novel, by Samuel P. Putnam. Cloth, $1.00. Paper, 50 cts.

WAKEMAN-MITCHELL DEBATE. Paper, 25 cts; cloth, 50cts. WAKEMAN'S ADDRESS only. Paper, 15 cents.

WOMAN SUFFRAGE, by J. G. Hertwig. Paper, 10 cents.

WORKS BY PROF. WILLIAM DENTON.

Be Thyself. Price, 10 cents.

Christianity no Finality; or, Spiritualism Superior to Christianity. Price, 10 cents.

Common Sense Thoughts on the Bible. Price, 10 cts.

Garrison in Heaven. A Dream. Price, 10 cents.

Geology: The Past and Future of our Planet. Price, $1.50.

Is Spiritualism True? Price, 10 cents.

Man's True Savior. Price, 10 cents.

Orthodoxy False, since Spiritualism is True. Price, 10 cents.

Radical Discourses on Religious Subjects. Price, $1.25.

Radical Rhymes. Price, $1.25.

Sermon from Shakspere's Text. Price, 10 cents.

Soul of Things; or, Psychometric Researches and Discoveries. In three volumes. Price; $1.50 per volume.

The Deluge in the Light of Modern Science. Price, 10 cents.

The God Proposed for Our National Constitution. Price, 10 cents.

The Irreconcilable Records; or, Genesis and Geology. Cloth, 40 cents; paper, 25 cents.

The Pocasset Tragedy. Price, 10 cents.

What is Right? Price, 10 cents.

What Was He; or, Jesus in the Light of the Nineteenth Century. Price, cloth, $1.25; paper, $1.

Who are Christians? Price, 10 cents.

Who Killed Mary Stannard? Price, 10 cents.

www.ingramcontent.com/pod-product-compliance
Lightning Source LLC
Chambersburg PA
CBHW021400230426
43666CB00006B/594